Peter Norton's
Computing Fundamentals

Interactive Browser Edition™ Student Guide

Third Edition

Glencoe
McGraw-Hill

New York, New York   Columbus, Ohio   Woodland Hills, California   Peoria, Illinois

Interactive Browser Edition™ Student Guide
Peter Norton's® Computing Fundamentals,
Third Edition

Glencoe/McGraw-Hill

A Division of The **McGraw·Hill** Companies

Part number: G04411.00

Send all inquiries to:

Glencoe/McGraw-Hill
8787 Orion Place
Columbus, OH 43240

2 3 4 5 6 7 8 9 10 066 03 02 01 00 99

CONTENTS

Thank you for choosing Peter Norton's® Introduction to Computers Interactive Browser Edition™. This Student Guide supplements the Interactive Browser Edition. Its purpose is to increase and strengthen your understanding of the material supplied in the Interactive Browser Edition CD-ROM. You should use this Student Guide to reinforce important concepts as you navigate the Interactive Browser Edition. In addition, the Student Guide will aid you in tracking your progress through the Interactive Browser Edition.

Each chapter of this Student Guide features a Hands-On Activities section. This section contains helpful review questions and discussion topics for you to complete. These questions complement the end-of-chapter review in the Interactive Browser Edition CD-ROM. It is recommended that you complete these sections and submit them to your instructor for review. Thus, your instructor is able to gauge your comprehension of the material as the course progresses.

A NOTE ON LAB SITUATIONS

The Interactive Browser Edition provides Bookmark and Notes features. If you are using this product in a lab, or on a computer other than your own, you may wish to save your bookmarks and notes to a floppy disk. This will allow you to retain your notes and bookmarks as you move from computer to computer. It is important that you become familiar with this feature, since you will lose these settings if they are not saved to a floppy disk or other transportable media.

In order to save the bookmarks and notes, click on the Bookmarks or Notes button on the toolbar, click on the Save As button, and point to the drive where the floppy disk or other media is located.

To load a set of previously saved bookmarks or notes: click the Bookmark or Notes button, then click the Open button, point to the drive that contains the media, select the file on the media, and click Open.

The following individuals contributed to the content and development of this program: L. Joyce Arntson, Robert Goldhamer, Jeanne Massingill, Pat Fenton, Rob Tidrow, Cheri Manning, Chris Ewald, Geneil Breeze, Bill McManus, Elliot Linzer, Jose Lozano, Cynthia Karrasch, Mary Sheskey, and Kurt Hampe. Special thanks goes to the following at Glencoe/McGraw-Hill whose dedication and hard work made this project possible: Corinne Gindroz, Janet Coulon, Bruce Albrecht, Hal Sturrock, Janet Grau, Sarah O'Donnell, Julia Holsclaw, Rachel Laskowski, Kim Harvey, and Denise Phillips. A personal thanks to Gary Schwartz, Satbir Bedi, Colleen Morrissey, Chris Shira, and Dave Kunkler. Finally, it was a privilege to work with Charles T. Huddleston without whose hard work, patience, and professionalism this project would not have become a reality.

October 1998

USING THE INTERACTIVE BROWSER EDITION AND STUDENT GUIDE

Each chapter of this *Student Guide* corresponds to a chapter on the Interactive Browser Edition.

Each chapter of this book has two major sections:

- ■ "Key Concepts" provides an overview of the terms and concepts covered in the chapter.
- ■ "Hands-On Activities" leads you through the chapter on the disk. This section also provides review questions that ensure that you have covered all the information provided in the chapter. Use these questions not only to test your knowledge, but as a guide; for example, if you cannot answer a question, you may need to go back to an earlier part of the chapter and review it.

Begin each chapter by reviewing the "Key Concepts" section. Afterward, launch the Interactive Browser Edition, and work through the chapter as directed in the "Hands-On Activities" section, answering the review questions as you go.

Launching the Interactive Browser Edition CD-ROM

The *Student Guide* assumes that you (or your instructor) have run the installation program on the disk. If not, please do so at this time.

To launch the Interactive Browser Edition from the CD, take the following steps:

1_ Place the compact disk in your computer's CD-ROM drive. If AutoPlay is enabled on your computer, the Interactive Browser Edition will start automatically, its main menu appearing in a customized window of your Web browser.

2_ If AutoPlay is not enabled, take the following steps:

    a. Click the Start button.
    b. From the Start menu, choose Programs.
    c. From the Programs menu, choose the title of the CD-ROM.
    d. From the submenu, choose Introduction to Computers, Computing Fundamentals, or Essential Concepts. Your Web browser will open, then a customized browser window will appear, displaying the Interactive Browser Edition's main menu.

From this menu, you can go to any chapter of the book by clicking its name or number. When you do, the selected chapter opens with a list of learning objectives and a navigation menu. The navigation menu provides links to each section and subsection in the chapter. More information on navigating the Interactive Browser is available in appendix C.

The Interactive Browser Edition's main menu.

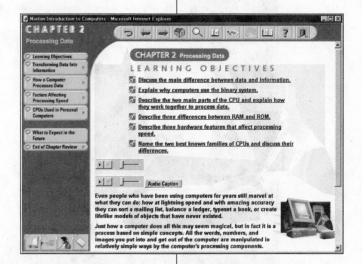

The opening screen for Chapter 2 of the Interactive Browser Edition. Each chapter provides a navigation menu on the left, which stays visible while you are working in the chapter.

PART

1

HOW COMPUTERS WORK

PART 1   HOW COMPUTERS WORK

The Amazing Computer

OBJECTIVES

When you complete this chapter, you will be able to do the following:

- List at least five professions in which computers are routinely used, and describe at least one of the ways computers have affected the work of people in those professions.
- List the four parts of a computer system.
- Identify four kinds of computer hardware.
- List the two major categories of software and explain the purpose of each.
- List the four most common types of computers available today and describe what kind of job each does best.

You can safely say that no other machine has had as great an impact on civilization as the computer, at least not since the invention of the printing press. This claim is supported by the fact that computers have taken on a role in nearly every aspect of our lives. Explore nearly any field of endeavor—from agriculture to brain surgery, from construction to zoology—and you will find that computers are there, and becoming more essential every day.

Although it may seem that computers are everywhere already, their use is still spreading rapidly, especially in the workplace. Every day, small business owners install new systems—even the long-time holdouts who never thought they would need a computer. Large companies are continually increasing the number and power of their computing systems, automating their business processes, developing new products on the computer, and selling their products and services on the Internet. This is why it is important that you become familiar with computers, their underlying technology, and their myriad uses.

In this chapter, you will see some of the many ways people use computers in daily life. You will also take a peek under the hood of these magnificent machines to see what makes them tick. Finally, you will learn about the various types of computers and which tasks each does best.

Perhaps no area of science has benefited more from computer technology—or contributed more to its development—than the space program.

NORTON Online
For information on the **history of the personal computer**, visit this book's Web site at **www.glencoe.com/norton/online**

KEY CONCEPTS

The number of uses for computers seems almost limitless. To develop a real appreciation of this amazing machine, it helps to get a sampling of the many ways computers are being applied in business, government, education, and many other walks of life. To understand how computers can perform so many tasks, you need to explore the basic hardware components that make computers tick, and the software that tells computers what to do.

The Multipurpose Tool

■ The first modern computers were massive, special-purpose machines. They were initially designed for use by the government and military, but quickly were adopted by large companies for business uses.

■ Modern medicine uses computers in many ways. For example, computers are used to assist in surgical procedures and to diagnose illnesses.

■ Educators are interested in computers as tools for interactive learning. Advances in computer and communication technology have brought the Internet and its resources to the classroom.

■ Computers are used in the manufacturing process to run complicated machines, perform repetitive tasks, and even manage parts of the process.

■ Engineers and architects use computers to design objects and structures with the help of CAD tools and techniques.

■ Attorneys use computers to access databases that contain records of old cases and data related to current ones.

■ The government is a major user of computers; many governmental agencies (such as the Internal Revenue Service, the Federal Bureau of Investigation, the Library of Congress, and even the White House) host their own World Wide Web sites.

■ Using computers and instruments equipped with a Musical Instrument Digital Interface (MIDI), musicians can combine or create sounds electronically, either in the recording studio or during live performances.

This police officer is using a mobile data terminal (MDT), which provides access to information such as license plate numbers of stolen cars. Computers have enabled law enforcement agencies to share data about crimes, criminals, and police activity around the nation.

■ Filmmakers use computers to create special effects. For example, the tornadoes in
Twister, the dinosaurs in *Jurassic Park*, and
the aliens in *Men in Black* were created
using computer software, and blended into
the final scenes. To make some computer-
generated characters (such as monsters or
aliens) move in a lifelike way, animators use
motion-capture technology to record the
movements of a real person or animal. The
computer can then assign those motions to
an animated character.

AN OVERVIEW OF THE COMPUTER SYSTEM

■ Computer systems include hardware, software, data, and people.

■ Hardware consists of electronic devices—the parts you can see and touch, such as the
keyboard, the system unit, or the monitor. The internal parts of a computer, such as disk
drives, modems, and processors, are hardware, too. Peripheral devices, such as printers
and scanners, are also hardware.

■ Software, also known as programs, consists of organized sets of instructions for controlling the computer.

■ Data consists of text, numbers, sounds, and images that the computer can manipulate.

■ People who use computers (users) also make up part of the computer system.

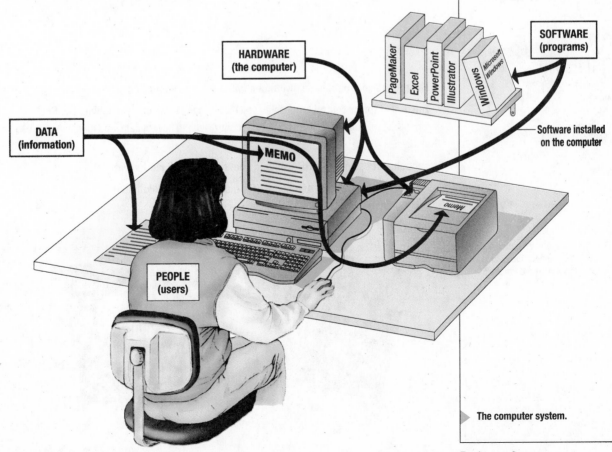

The computer system.

Looking Inside the Machine

■ The hardware—that is, the physical components—of a computer falls into four categories: processor, memory, input and output (I/O) devices, and storage.

Types of hardware devices. ◄

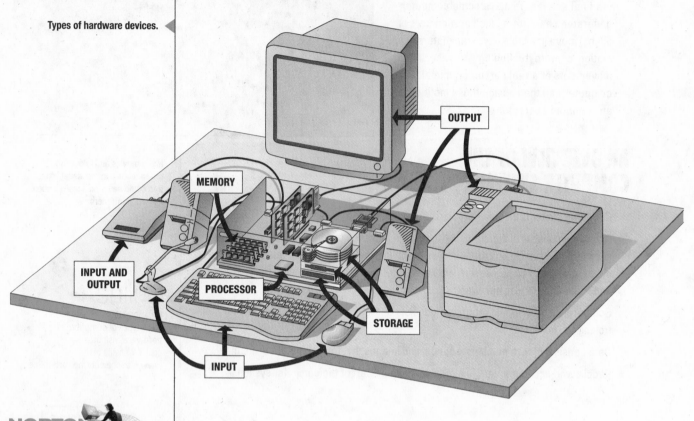

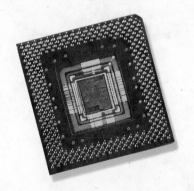

NORTON Online

For information on **computer processors**, visit this book's Web site at **www.glencoe.com/norton/online**

■ The processing function is divided between the processor and memory.

■ The processor, or central processing unit (CPU), is the brain of the machine. The CPU performs several functions, processing data, controlling the flow of data, and managing the use of devices.

■ Random access memory (RAM) holds data as the CPU works with it.

■ The most common units of measure for memory are the kilobyte (KB), megabyte (MB), and gigabyte (GB).

The CPU of a modern computer is a tiny device. The chip is about the size of a thumbnail. ◄

- The role of input is to provide the computer with data from the user or some other source. The keyboard, mouse, and scanner are commonly used input devices.

- The function of output is to present processed data to the user. The monitor and printer are the most common output devices.

- Communication devices perform both input and output, allowing computers to share information with one another. Modems and network interface card are examples of devices that perform both input and output.

- Storage devices, such as disks, hold data that is not currently being used by the CPU.

Software Brings the Machine to Life

- Programs are electronic instructions that tell the computer how to accomplish certain tasks.

- When a computer is using a particular program, it is said to be running or executing the program.

- The operating system tells the computer how to interact with the user and how to use the hardware devices that are attached to the computer.

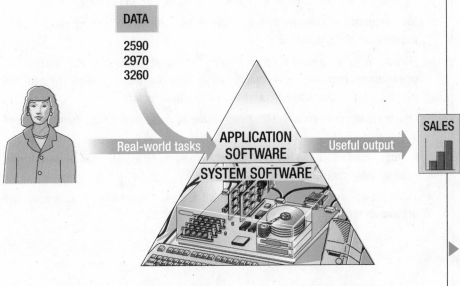

DATA
2590
2970
3260

Real-world tasks → APPLICATION SOFTWARE / SYSTEM SOFTWARE → Useful output → SALES

▶ Application software and system software.

- Application software tells the computer how to accomplish tasks the user requires.

- Seven important kinds of application software are word processing programs, databases, spreadsheets, graphics, education and entertainment applications, utilities, and communication programs.

The Shapes of Computers Today

- There are four types of computers: supercomputers, mainframes, minicomputers, and microcomputers.

- Supercomputers are the most powerful computers in terms of processing. They are useful for problems requiring complex calculations.

- Mainframe computers, which generally have many terminals connected to a single, large computer, handle massive amounts of input, output, and storage.

- Minicomputers are smaller than mainframes but larger than microcomputers. They usually have multiple terminals.

- Microcomputers are more commonly known as personal computers (PC). The term *PC* often denotes microcomputers that are either IBM-PCs or compatibles. The term can also refer to personal computers made by other manufacturers.

- Desktop computers, including the newer tower models, are the most common type of personal computer.

- Laptops (notebooks) and personal digital assistants (PDAs) are used by people who need portable computing power outside the office.

- The most powerful microcomputers, which are used by engineers, scientists, and graphic artists, are known as workstations.

HANDS On Activities

HARDWARE AND SOFTWARE WORKING TOGETHER

The Interactive Browser Edition introduces you to computer hardware and software and shows you how the two work together. As you work through Chapter 1 of the Interactive Browser Edition, you will learn about the basic hardware components that are required for a fully functioning computer, and you will see the role software plays in getting the computer to perform specific tasks. You also will learn about the many types of computers in use today, and the specific uses for each type of computer system.

The following sections are designed to help you navigate Chapter 1. As you work through the chapter, be sure to answer the review questions on the following pages. Write your answers directly in this book.

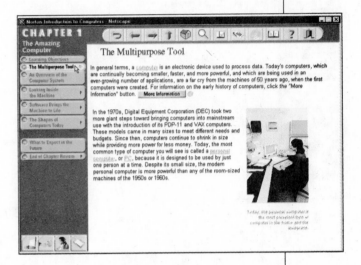

The Multipurpose Tool

It would take months to explore the myriad ways computers are being used today. People in all walks of life are increasingly using computers to help them find information, track their activities, share information and ideas, and much more. Computers help us design rockets and catch criminals, communicate across vast distances and create works of art.

From the navigation menu on the left side of your browser window, choose The Multipurpose Tool. Use this menu item's options to explore this section of the chapter. As you work through this section, answer the following questions:

1. Today, the most common type of computer you will see is called a _____ , or

   _____ .

2. Portable personal computers are also known as _____ or

   _____ .

3. _____ is the process of working at home or on the road and having access to a work computer via telecommunications equipment, such as modems and fax machines.

4. Using _____ tools, architects and engineers can design buildings, products, and other objects.

5. Manufacturing with computers and robotics is called

_____ .

6. _____ is a standard that enables musicians to connect electronic instruments to one another or to a computer.

From the set of options under The Multi-purpose Tool, choose Self Check: Computers in Business. Complete the quiz on screen; follow the instructions on the screen as you go.

nORTON Notebook

Now, review this chapter's Norton Notebook section, which discusses Global Positioning Systems (GPS). List three potential uses for GPS.

1. _____

2. _____

3. _____

An Overview of the Computer System

Because computers are being applied to so many different tasks, they must take many different shapes. Remember that the computer sitting on your desk is only one type of computer. Others include the security systems that protect our homes and offices, appliances we use in our homes, and the systems that guide satellites through space. Even though computers take many forms, they share four common aspects, which you will explore in this section.

From the navigation menu on the left side of your browser window, choose An Overview of the Computer System. As you work through this section, answer the following questions:

1. The term _____ refers to the computer itself.

2. The system converts _____ into information.

3. The terms _____ and _____ refer to sets of electronic instructions that tell the hardware what to do.

Techview

Now, review this chapter's Techview section, which discusses world chess champion Garry Kasparov's second match against the chess-playing computer, Big Blue. In your opinion, was the match a fair one? Why or why not?

_____

_____

_____

Looking Inside the Machine

What will you find if you take the cover off a computer and look inside? The sheer number of components may seem intimidating, but all those parts are not completely separate and independent. They work together in groups to perform specific types of tasks, and therefore can be categorized. This makes the computer easier to understand. In this section, you will learn about the major categories of hardware that make up a computer system.

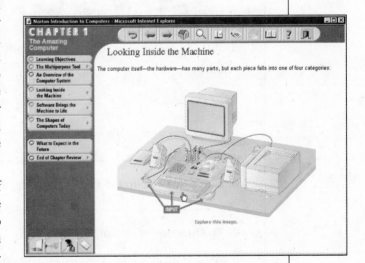

From the navigation menu on the left side of your browser window, choose Looking Inside the Machine. Use this menu item's options to explore this section of the chapter. As you work through this section, answer the following questions:

1. Each piece of computer hardware falls into one of these four categories:

_____ , _____ ,

_____ , and _____ .

2. The complex procedure that transforms raw data into useful information is called

_____ .

3. A computer's processor usually consists of one or more _____ ,
which are plugged into a circuit board called the _____ .

4. What three terms are commonly used to measure the large amounts of data stored in
RAM? How much data does each term represent, in bytes?

_____

_____

_____

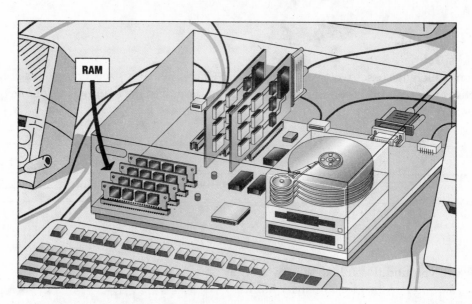

5. Why do new generations of PCs usually feature more RAM than previous generations
did?

_____

_____

_____

6. Name three examples of an input device: _____ ,
_____ , and _____ .

7. The function of an output device is to _____ .

8. What is the purpose of an input/output (I/O) device? Give two examples of an I/O device.

_____

_____

9. Three types of storage media commonly used in computers are

_____ ,

_____ , and

_____ .

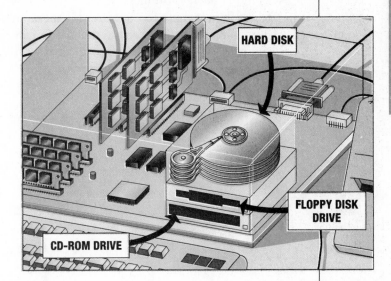

10. What are the differences between memory and storage in a computer?

_____

_____

_____

11. How much data can a typical compact disk hold?

_____

From the set of options under Looking Inside the Machine, choose Self Check: Input Devices. Complete the quiz on screen; follow the instructions on the screen as you go.

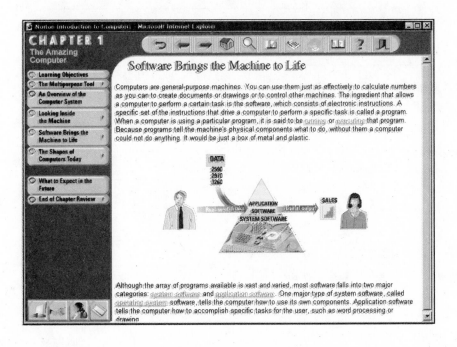

Software Brings the Machine to Life

If the processor is the computer's brain and the hardware is its bones, then the software is its muscles. Software tells the computer what to do and how to do it. Without software installed and operational, a computer cannot do anything. This section introduces you to the two primary categories of computer software and gives examples from each category. You will also learn where the computer gets different types of instructions, and the types of tasks software and the user can make the computer perform.

From the navigation menu on the left side of your browser window, choose Software Brings the Machine to Life. Use this menu item's options to explore this section of the chapter. As you work through this section, answer the following questions:

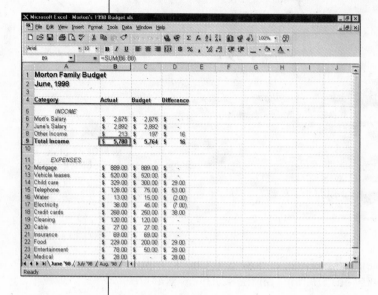

1. The two major categories of software are
_____ and
_____ .

2. When the computer is using a program, it is said to be
_____ or
_____
the program.

3. Describe the three steps involved in the startup process, which takes place when you turn on a computer.

_____

_____

_____

_____

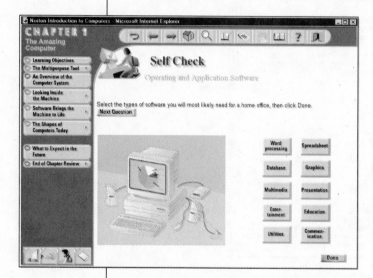

4. What does application software do?

_____

_____

_____

_____

_____

_____

_____

_____

5. Give three examples of application software: _____ ,
_____ , and _____ .

From the set of options under Software Brings the Machine to Life, choose Self Check: Operating and Application Software. Complete the quiz on screen; follow the instructions on the screen as you go.

The Shapes of Computers Today

A few years ago, there were only a few types of computers that one might recognize—most of which were very large, slow, and dedicated to a single purpose. Today, the number of computing options is mind-boggling, for the individual user as well as the corporation that purchases thousands of systems each year. Further, new types of computer systems are being developed every few years, and current systems are rapidly evolving in size and shape, as well as in features and capabilities. This section introduces you to the basic categories of computers used in homes and businesses today, and explains the differences among them.

From the navigation menu on the left side of your browser window, choose The Shapes of Computers Today. Use this menu item's options to explore this section of the chapter. As you work through this section, answer the following questions:

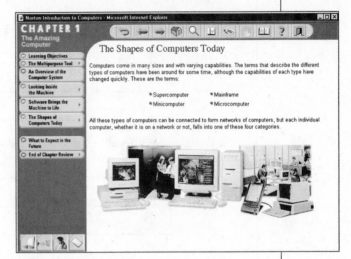

1. General-purpose computers fall into four categories, which are

   _____,

   _____,

   _____, and

   _____.

2. The most powerful computers built today

   are _____.

3. A(n) _____ is a large, multiuser computer system designed to handle massive amounts of input, output, and storage, and which usually is composed of a powerful CPU connected to many terminals.

4. What is a terminal?

_____

_____

_____

5. Today's microcomputers have at least _____ times as much storage capacity and operate at least _____ times faster than the original PCs did.

6. Why do some people consider it misleading to refer to a Macintosh computer as a "PC"?

_____

_____

_____

7. What is the difference between a desktop PC and a tower PC?

_____

_____

_____

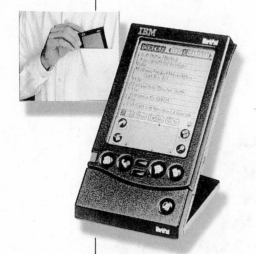

8. The _____ (also called a _____) is the smallest of portable computers.

9. A handheld computer is like a personal digital assistant, but features a _____ .

10. The most powerful type of personal computer is the _____ .

Productivity Tip

Now, review this chapter's Productivity Tip section, which discusses choosing the right type of computer for your profession. What type of computer do you think would be most useful to you in your chosen career? Explain your reasons for choosing a specific type of computer.

_____

_____

_____

What to Expect in the Future

Computers are affecting our lives and work in an ever-growing number of ways. Given the fact that computers are used in nearly every profession, it is increasingly likely that you will need to master some computer skills. Even if these new skills are not required in your career, you may want to use a computer at home—for shopping, doing school-work, investing, and so on. Regardless, computer technology is bound to creep into your life in some way.

From the navigation menu on the left side of your browser window, choose What to Expect in the Future. Study the discussion and answer the following questions:

1. Does your current job require you to use a computer? If not, do you think that a future job will require you to use one?

_____

_____

_____

2. What specific computer skills do you hope to master? How will these computer skills affect or enhance your career?

_____

_____

_____

3. Does the Internet (or a smaller computer network) affect the way you use your com-puter now? If so, how? How will the explosion in connectivity affect the way you use the computer?

_____

_____

_____

Computers
In Your Career

Now, review this chapter's Computers in Your Career section, which discusses the ways in which the technologies covered in this chapter could affect your career. In the space provided here, describe the area of technology that you think might most affect your career, and explain why:

_____

_____

_____

_____

_____

_____

_____

_____

_____

_____

_____

_____

_____

_____

_____

_____

_____

_____

_____

_____

_____

End of Chapter Review

The End of Chapter Review section is designed to refresh you on the major points presented in this chapter, and to test your understanding of the information.

From the navigation menu on the left side of your browser window, choose End of Chapter Review. Use the menu item's options to review the Visual Summary sections for this chapter, review the chapter's Key Terms, and take the end-of-chapter quizzes.

VISUAL SUMMARIES

Review each of this chapter's Visual Summaries in turn. Each Visual Summary provides a quick overview of the major points in each section of the chapter. If you want more information about any item in a Visual Summary, click the link button next to that item, and you will return to the full discussion of that topic. (Then choose the Go Back button to return to the Visual Summary.)

KEY TERMS

Choose the Key Terms option if you need to find the definition for any of the important terms or concepts introduced in this chapter. To get a definition for a term, simply look up the term in the list and click it. The term's definition will appear in a separate window. Use this section to prepare yourself for the Key Term Quiz.

KEY TERM QUIZ

Complete the Key Term Quiz on your screen. You complete the quiz on screen, in crossword-puzzle form. When you are done with the test, choose the Solve button at the bottom of the screen. If you want to start over, choose the Reset button to clear your responses and then start again.

REVIEW QUESTIONS

Complete the Review Questions on your screen. You complete the quiz by typing correct responses in the blanks provided, selecting responses from a list, or by selecting option buttons. When you are done with the test, choose the Done button at the bottom of the screen. If you want to start over, choose the Reset button to clear your responses and then start again.

DISCUSSION QUESTIONS

Complete the Discussion Questions on your screen. You complete the quiz by typing your answers in the text boxes provided. When you are done with the test, you can print your answers and give them to your instructor. Your instructor may choose to discuss these questions in class.

*inter*NET Workshop

Do the exercises described in the Internet Workshop section. Write your findings in the spaces provided here.

1. How many Web sites did you find containing historical information about early computers? List the URLs of the sites here, along with a brief summary of the information they provided.

_____

_____

_____

_____

_____

2. How many Web sites did you find that provided up-to-the-minute information about computers and technology? List the name and URL of each site here.

_____

_____

_____

_____

_____

3. How many online newspapers did you find on the Web? List the name and URL of each site here.

_____

_____

_____

_____

4. How many Web sites did you find that are devoted to space exploration? List the name and URL of each site here.

_____

_____

_____

_____

_____

CHAPTER 2

Processing Data

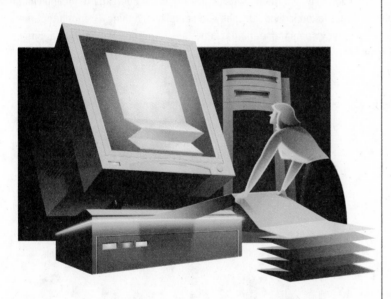

OBJECTIVES

When you complete this chapter, you will be able to do the following:

- **Discuss the main difference between data and information.**
- **Explain why computers use the binary system.**
- **Describe the two main parts of the CPU and explain how they work together to process data.**
- **Describe three differences between RAM and ROM.**
- **Describe three hardware features that affect processing speed.**
- **Name the two best-known families of CPUs and list their differences.**

How does a computer do its job? When you are writing a letter, sorting a database, or calculating a budget, how does the computer work with data and turn it into information you can understand and use? The answers to these questions may surprise you. Even though a computer seems complex, it actually performs its functions by using some simple processes.

As you learned in Chapter 1, two of the computer's components work together to process data: the central processing unit (CPU) and memory. When you peek inside these components to see how they work, you will probably be surprised at their simplicity. In fact, computers process data by breaking it into a very simple set of codes. Because they have the internal resources to handle many of these codes at a time, the CPU and memory can process a tremendous amount of data very quickly. By continually improving the amount of data that CPUs can handle, computer makers increase the speed at which computers can operate.

In this chapter, you will find out what data is, how it differs from information, and what form it takes in the computer. You'll explore the computer's processing components and learn about important factors affecting a computer's speed. Finally, you will examine the microprocessors made by the biggest chip manufacturers.

NORTON
Online

For more information on **transistors**, visit
this book's Web site at
www.glencoe.com/norton/online

KEY CONCEPTS

To understand how a computer processes data, you need to look into the computer's "brain." Because any computer's brain is a collection of chips and the pathways that connect them, it isn't too difficult to understand. You also need to learn about the language a computer uses to express data—that is, how the computer takes letters and numbers that humans understand, and converts them into a digital form that it can understand.

Transforming Data into Information

▪ Although the words *data* and *information* are often used interchangeably, there is an important distinction between them. Data is like facts out of context, like the individual letters on this page. Taken individually, they do not tell you a thing. Grouped together, however, they convey specific meanings. Information, therefore, is individual bits of data put together within a context.

It is often necessary to distinguish between data and information.

DATA	INFORMATION
FACTS OUT OF CONTEXT	**MEANINGFUL COLLECTIONS OF DATA**

576-21-0102

#37

Felicia

Tone =

$39.70
$41.85
$16.19

Population estimates
Sockeye Salmon
Inverness Creek

Year	Est.
1991	16,500
1992	16,000
1993	17,000
1994	16,500
1995	19,200
1996	19,500
1997	19,000
1998	21,000
1999	20,400
2000	20,900

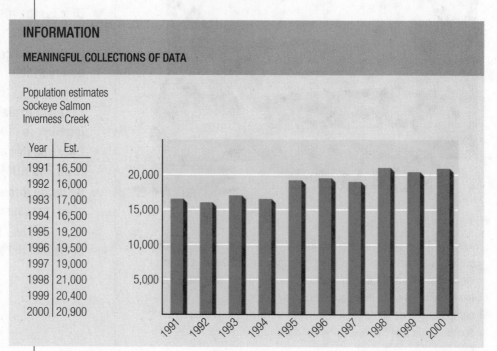

Computers represent data with electrical switches. An "on" switch represents a 1. An "off" switch represents a 0.

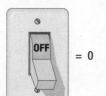

▪ Computers cannot understand or work with human language (that is, characters such as *T, e,* or *8*). Instead, the computer must take the letters, numbers, and other characters you provide and reduce them to digital data. To create digital data, the computer uses the binary number system.

▪ Binary numbers are simply a series of 1s and 0s, which to the computer represent "on" and "off," respectively. This is necessary because computer processing is performed by transistors that have only two possible states: on and off. To display information back to you, the computer must convert the binary numbers to characters that you understand, and then display them on the screen or send them to a printer.

- The binary numbering system works the same way as the decimal system, except it has only two available symbols: 0 and 1. The decimal system has ten available symbols: 0, 1, 2, 3, 4, 5, 6, 7, 8, and 9.

- A single unit of data is called a bit; eight bits make up one byte. The computer recognizes each character of data as one byte, which is a series of eight binary numbers. For example, this byte of binary numbers—0110 0101—represents the letter *e* to the computer. Therefore, if you type the letter *e* at the keyboard, the computer converts it to the byte 0110 0101.

- The computer uses code sets to determine how to convert human-language characters to binary characters and vice versa. A code set is a standard, which assigns a specific binary byte to each character that can be typed at the computer's keyboard. In the most common code set, ASCII, each character consists of one byte (eight bits) of data. There are several code sets, but ASCII is the most widely used, and has been modified to support several different human languages.

NORTON
Online
For more information on **computer memory**, visit this book's Web site at **www.glencoe.com/norton/online**

How a Computer Processes Data

- A microcomputer's processing is handled by the central processing unit (CPU) and memory.

- The CPU has two main parts: the control unit and the arithmetic logic unit (ALU).

- The CPU's control unit contains a built-in set of instructions, which are expressed in microcode. These instructions help the CPU translate and use the data and instructions that it receives from you and from software programs.

- The ALU can perform two basic processes: arithmetic processes and logical processes. Arithmetic processes involve simple arithmetic: addition, subtraction, multiplication, and division. Logical processes involve basic comparisons between different pieces of data, to determine whether they are the same or different in some way. The ALU includes a group of registers, which hold the data that is being processed.

- The CPU cannot hold all the data that it needs at any given time. Therefore, the computer also has built-in memory circuits. These memory circuits provide two types of storage—volatile and nonvolatile—and provide the CPU with instant access to the data it needs.

- Read-only memory (ROM) is nonvolatile; that is, ROM is permanent memory that stores data even when the computer's power is off. ROM is used to hold instructions that run the computer when the power is first turned on. The data in a computer's ROM never changes.

CPU

A personal computer's CPU is a single microprocessor, which is located on the computer's main circuit board—or motherboard.

ROM chip

ROM usually consists of a small chip, located near the CPU on the motherboard.

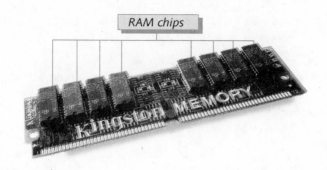

In personal computers, RAM chips are normally mounted on a small circuit board, which is plugged into the motherboard.

- Random-access memory (RAM) is volatile; that is, RAM is temporary memory that stores data only when the computer's power is on. The computer can write data to RAM as needed, and then erase it to make room for other data. The data in a computer's RAM changes very frequently while the computer is in use.

- A computer's memory chips can hold a great deal of data, and a method is required to keep track of each byte of data in memory, so the CPU can find the data it needs at any time. To accomplish this, each location in memory is assigned a unique number, called a memory address. The CPU uses these addresses to find data, just as you can use a street address to find a building in a large city.

Factors Affecting Processing Speed

- The more data a computer can process at one time, the faster the computer will operate. Several factors determine how fast a PC can process data.

- Speed is greatly affected by the amount of data that the computer's registers can hold. Older computers could process 16 bits of data at one time. (Thus, they were said to have a "word size" of 16 bits.) Current PCs can process 32 bits simultaneously; more powerful workstations can even process 64 bits simultaneously.

- RAM has a tremendous impact on a computer's speed. Generally speaking, the more RAM a computer has, the faster it can operate. This is because the CPU can keep more of the active program and data in memory, rather than in storage (a disk).

The CPU is attached to two kinds of memory: RAM, which is volatile, and ROM, which is nonvolatile.

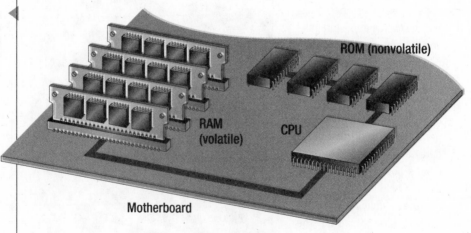

Usually, cache memory is visible on the motherboard as a group of chips next to the CPU.

■ The processing speed of the CPU is determined by its built-in clock. This internal clock sets the pace for the CPU by using a vibrating quartz crystal. The crystal's rate of vibration is measured in hertz, or cycles per second. These crystals can be made to vibrate very rapidly, to a current top speed of 400 million times per second, or 400 megahertz (400 MHz). Note that this speed will certainly increase as processor technology advances. In fact, it may have already increased by the time you read this. The faster a computer's internal clock is, the faster the computer can process data.

■ In a computer, a special pathway is required for data to travel from one component to another (from RAM to the CPU, for example). This pathway is called a bus. There are two kinds of buses: The data bus carries data between the CPU, memory, and other hardware devices on the motherboard. The address bus connects the CPU and memory, and carries only memory addresses, to help the CPU find data more quickly in memory. Both of the buses are located on the motherboard. The width of the data bus determines how many bits at a time can be transmitted between the CPU and other devices.

■ Cache memory is a type of high-speed memory that contains the most recent data and instructions that have been loaded by the CPU. Because the CPU can access cache memory faster than it can access RAM or a disk, a computer's operation can be boosted if cache memory is used. As with RAM, the more cache a computer has, the faster it can operate.

■ A CPU relies on a math coprocessor to perform the sophisticated calculations required by many software programs. By delegating complex mathematical operations to a separate processor, the CPU can spend its time performing other operations. For this reason, a math coprocessor (or floating-point unit, as it is also called) can greatly enhance a computer's performance, especially if the system runs complex math-based programs (such as CAD programs or 3-D rendering programs, large databases, or spreadsheets).

Intel's first microprocessor, the 4004.

NORTON Online

For more information on **Intel**, visit this book's Web site at **www.glencoe.com/norton/online**

Intel's latest microprocessor, the Pentium II.

A RISC chip from NEC, the VR4111 processor.

CPUs Used in Personal Computers

■ Most of the world's personal computers (except Macintosh computers) are controlled by processors made by Intel. Intel's first microprocessor, the 4004, was used in the first electronic calculators. Since 1978, Intel's processors have evolved from the 8086 and the 8088 to the 80286, the 80386, the 80486, the Pentium, the Pentium Pro, and the Pentium II.

■ Intel competitors, AMD and Cyrix, make the processors that are commonly found in low-end, low-priced (under $1,000) consumer and home PCs. Their processors are designed to provide the same features as Intel's processors, with comparable performance at a lower price.

■ Motorola makes the CPUs used in Macintosh and PowerPC computers: the 68000, 68020, 68030, and 68040 are for Macintoshes; the PowerPC series is now used in the Power Macintoshes.

■ Reduced instruction set computing (RISC) chips use smaller instruction sets than those used by standard PC microprocessor chips, so that each instruction executes more quickly. Some high-end microcomputers—called workstations—and mid-size computers use RISC chips, as well as a growing number of PCs. Most PCs utilize more complex instruction sets, and therefore are based on complex instruction set computing (CISC) chips.

HANDS On Activities

THE CPU, MEMORY, AND DATA PROCESSING

The Interactive Browser Edition contains a great deal of information about the way computers process and understand data, and shows you how the computer translates data into information that humans can understand. As you work through Chapter 2 of the Interactive Browser Edition, you also will find demonstrations that show you how the binary number system works, the differences between processors, and more.

The following sections are designed to help you navigate Chapter 2. As you work through the chapter, answer the review questions on the following pages. Write your answers directly in this book.

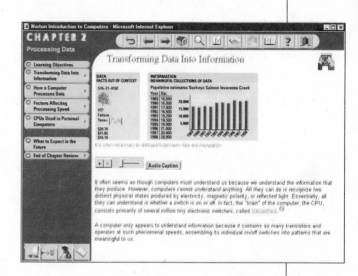

Transforming Data into Information

It is important to note that computers cannot understand anything. They can only take the literal instructions they receive from a user or a program and follow those instructions to achieve a specific result. It is also important to note that data—the isolated bits of information that a computer understands—is different from information, which is a collection of data presented within a context that makes it meaningful to people.

From the navigation menu on the left side of your browser window, choose Transforming Data into Information. Use this menu item's options to explore this section of the chapter. As you work through this section, answer the following questions:

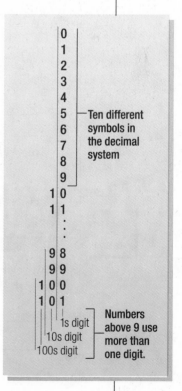

H	0100 1000
e	0110 0101
r	0111 0010
e	0110 0101
	0010 0000
a	0110 0001
r	0111 0010
e	0110 0101
	0010 0000
s	0111 0011
o	0110 1111
m	0110 1101
e	0110 0101
	0010 0000
w	0111 0111
o	0110 1111
r	0111 0010
d	0110 0100
s	0111 0011
.	0010 0001

1. The CPU consists primarily of several million tiny electronic switches, called _____ .

2. _____ is the term used to describe the information represented by groups of on/off switches.

3. What is the difference between the decimal system and the binary system? Which system is used by computers to represent data?

_____

_____

_____

4. A(n) _____ is the amount of memory required to store a single character, and is comprised of eight

_____ .

5. From the Transforming Data into Information menu option, choose Bits and Bytes. Working with the ASCII code table, if necessary, set the switches to create the following characters, and write the correct switch settings for each character:

```
1 bit
 ↓
 0  0  0  0  0  0  0  0  =
[ ][ ][ ][ ][ ][ ][ ][ ]
off off off off off off off off
◄———— 8 bits = 1 byte ————►
Decimal Equivalent: [0          ]
Character: [Null       ]
```

8 = _ _ _ _ _ _ _ _

h = _ _ _ _ _ _ _ _

E = _ _ _ _ _ _ _ _

q = _ _ _ _ _ _ _ _

P = _ _ _ _ _ _ _ _

% = _ _ _ _ _ _ _ _

. = _ _ _ _ _ _ _ _

6. _____ , _____ , and _____ are three of the most popular systems in which numbers represent letters of the alphabet, punctuation marks, and other symbols.

NORTON *Notebook*

Now, review this chapter's Norton Notebook section, which discusses dive computers. Name three tasks a dive computer can perform or assist a diver in performing:

1. _____

2. _____

3. _____

How a Computer Processes Data

Several components are involved in the processing of data, and each component serves a specific function. The computer assigns a different type of resource to each stage in the processing of data; this allocation of resources enables computers to operate faster and more efficiently.

From the navigation menu on the left side of your browser window, choose How a Computer Processes Data. Use this menu item's options to explore this section of the chapter. As you work through this section, answer the following questions:

1. The _____ and _____ handle processing in a computer.

2. _____ is the ability of a hardware device or a software product to interact successfully with all succeeding versions of software or hardware.

3. In a microcomputer, the entire CPU is contained on a tiny chip called a _____ .

4. All the computer's resources are managed from the _____ , the logical hub of the computer.

5. The computer's CPU is attached to two types of memory: _____ and _____ .

6. What is the difference between volatile memory and nonvolatile memory?

_____

_____

_____

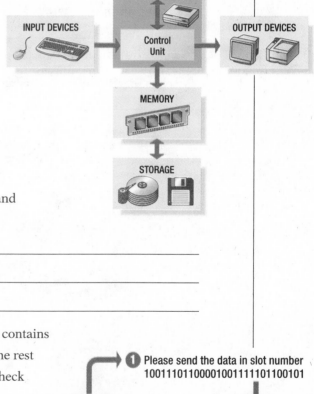

7. Among other things, _____ contains a set of start-up instructions, which ensure that the rest of the system's memory is functioning properly, check for hardware devices, and check for an operating system on the computer's disk drives.

8. There are several types of RAM used in computers: _____ and _____ are two of them.

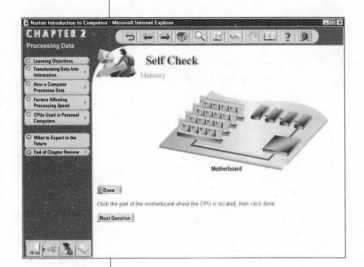

From the set of options under How a Computer Processes Data, choose Self Check: Memory. Complete the quiz on screen; follow the instructions on the screen as you go.

Factors Affecting Processing Speed

The computer's CPU alone does not determine how fast the system operates. Instead, a number of components work together to enable a computer to operate at top speed. If any one of these components fails or is not well matched to other parts of the system, then overall performance will suffer.

From the navigation menu on the left side of your browser window, choose Factors Affecting Processing Speed. Use this menu item's options to explore this section of the chapter. As you work through this section, answer the following questions:

1. _____ states that CPU computing power doubles every 18 months.

2. A computer's _____—the size of the registers in the CPU—determines the amount of data the computer can work with at any given time.

3. When the computer needs access to other parts of a program on the disk, it can

   _____ nonessential parts from RAM back to the hard disk and

   _____ the program code or data it needs.

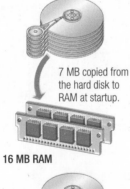

7 MB copied from the hard disk to RAM at startup.

16 MB RAM

With more RAM available, more of the operating system can be loaded from the hard disk at startup.

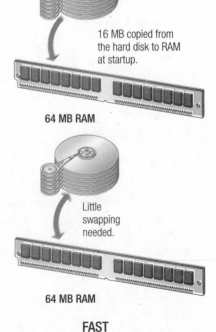

16 MB copied from the hard disk to RAM at startup.

64 MB RAM

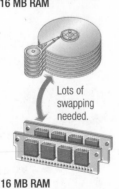

Lots of swapping needed.

16 MB RAM

SLOW

If more of the operating system can be loaded into RAM, then less needs to be swapped while the computer is runnnng.

The hard disk is much slower than RAM, so less swapping makes for a faster computer.

Little swapping needed.

64 MB RAM

FAST

4. One _____ means the time it takes to turn a transistor off and back on again.

5. A computer's clock speed is measured in _____ , which is the frequency of electrical vibrations, or cycles per second. The term _____ means "millions of cycles per second."

6. The number of wires in a computer's _____ determines the speed at which data is transmitted between the computer's components.

7. Why is a 32-bit bus preferable to an 8-bit bus?

_____

_____

_____

_____

_____

_____

8. The _____ connects the CPU and memory, and is used only to transmit _____ .

9. How does cache memory help a computer run faster?

_____

_____

_____

_____

_____

_____

10. A(n) _____ is a chip that is specially designed to handle compli-cated mathematical operations.

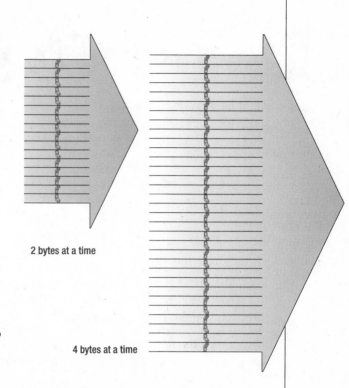

2 bytes at a time

4 bytes at a time

1 Please send the data in slot number
1001110110000100111110110 0101

ADDRESS BUS

CPU

DATA BUS

RAM

2 OK, here it comes.
01001100

Productivity Tip

Now, review this chapter's Productivity Tip section, which discusses upgrading your PC for better performance. Name three ways you can quickly upgrade a PC:

1. _____

2. _____

3. _____

CPUs Used in Personal Computers

Different types of computers are built around specific types of CPUs. The CPU at the heart of IBM-compatible PCs, for example, is different from the CPU that runs Macintosh computers. Other types of CPUs are used by PowerPCs and workstations.

From the navigation menu on the left side of your browser window, choose CPUs Used in Personal Computers. Use this menu item's options to explore this section of the chapter. As you work through this section, answer the following questions:

1. The family of Intel chips used in PCs—from the 8086 to the Pentium II—is often referred to as the _____ line.

2. Pentium II's architecture includes an amazing _____ transistors.

3. The Intel _____ microprocessor was the first to combine a processor, a math coprocessor, and a cache memory controller on a single chip.

4. Introduced with the Pentium, the MMX _____ enables one instruction to perform the same function on multiple pieces of data.

5. _____ and _____ are the two main competitors to Intel's dominance.

6. Apple's Macintosh computers are based on chips manufactured by _____ .

7. Explain the basic difference between complex instruction set computing (CISC) processors and reduced instruction set computing (RISC) processors.

_____

_____

_____

8. Some companies are developing computers with thousands of microprocessors, known as

_____ .

From the set of options under CPUs Used in Personal Computers, choose Self Check: Processor Chips. Complete the quiz on screen: follow the instructions on the screen as you go.

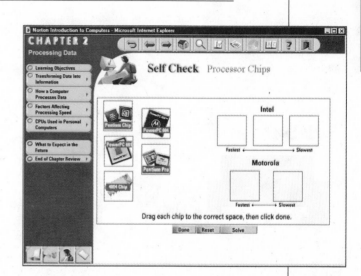

Techview

Now, review this chapter's Techview section, which discusses parallel processing. In the space provided here, explain why parallel processing is becoming more important for large organizations:

_____

_____

_____

What To Expect in the Future

We have come to expect great things from the computer industry, but the most tremendous advances would not be possible without continued improvements to the basic technology that enables our computers to operate. This includes enhancements to processor speed and capacity, new ways to squeeze more transistors onto shrinking chips, and much more.

From the navigation menu on the left side of your browser window, choose What to Expect in the Future. After reading this section, answer the following questions:

1. If Moore's Law holds true through the year 2015, how fast should PC processors be at that time?

_____

2. What two technological developments may make the greatest impact on computing in the near future?

_____ and _____

3. Describe the significant advances of the Merced chip.

_____

_____

_____

Computers
In Your Career

Now, review this chapter's Computers in Your Career section, which discusses the ways in which the technologies covered in this chapter could affect your career. In the space provided here, describe the area of technology that you think might most affect your career, and explain why:

_____

_____

_____

_____

_____

_____

_____

_____

_____

_____

_____

_____

_____

_____

End of Chapter Review

The End of Chapter Review section is designed to refresh you on the major points presented in this chapter, and to test your understanding of the information.

From the navigation menu on the left side of your browser window, choose End of Chapter Review. Use the menu item's options to review the Visual Summary sections for this chapter, review the chapter's Key Terms, and take the end-of-chapter quizzes.

VISUAL SUMMARIES

Review each of this chapter's Visual Summaries in turn. Each Visual Summary provides a quick overview of the major points in each section of the chapter. If you want more information about any item in a Visual Summary, click the link button next to that item, and you will return to the full discussion of that topic. (Then choose the Go Back button to return to the Visual Summary.)

KEY TERMS

Choose the Key Terms option if you need to find the definition for any of the important terms or concepts introduced in this chapter. To get a definition for a term, simply look up the term in the list and click it. The term's definition will appear in a separate window. Use this section to prepare yourself for the Key Term Quiz.

KEY TERM QUIZ

Complete the Key Term Quiz on your screen. You complete the quiz on screen, in crossword-puzzle form. When you are done with the test, choose the Solve button at the bottom of the screen. If you want to start over, choose the Reset button to clear your responses and then start again.

REVIEW QUESTIONS

Complete the Review Questions on your screen. You complete the quiz by typing correct responses in the blanks provided, selecting responses from a list, or by selecting option buttons. When you are done with the test, choose the Done button at the bottom of the screen. If you want to start over, choose the Reset button to clear your responses and then start again.

DISCUSSION QUESTIONS

Complete the Discussion Questions on your screen. You complete the quiz by typing your answers in the text boxes provided. When you are done with the test, you can print your answers and give them to your instructor. Your instructor may choose to discuss these questions in class.

*inter*NET Workshop

Do the exercises described in the Internet Workshop section. Write your findings in the spaces provided here.

1. Which Web sites, if any, can you find that describe new innovations in CPU design?

_____

_____

_____

_____

2. How do competitors of Intel describe their products? Summarize your findings here.

_____

_____

_____

_____

3. Can you find any charts that show performance of Pentium chips against other chips? If so, print them out and give them to your instructor. Be sure to note the URL where you found the information.

_____

_____

_____

4. Can you find a Web site that discusses the Unicode Worldwide Character Standard? If so, write down the site's URL.

_____

5. List the names and URLs of Web sites you can find that sell the following PC components:

■ CPU upgrades: _____

_____

■ Motherboards: _____

_____

■ Cache memory: _____

_____

■ Memory (RAM): _____

_____

CHAPTER 3

Interacting with Your Computer

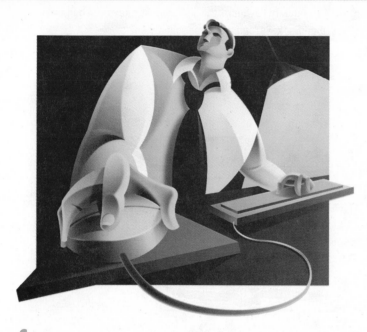

OBJECTIVES

When you complete this chapter, you will be able to do the following:

- **List at least three common input and output devices.**
- **Name the processes a video monitor uses to display images.**
- **Name the components of a mouse and list the common techniques used to maintain a mouse.**
- **Name three types of printers and list the advantages and disadvantages of each.**
- **Explain how input and output devices communicate with the other parts of the computer.**

So far, you have focused on the computer's internal components and the principles on which the machine operates. Although it is essential to understand these internal aspects of the computer, you don't work with them every day. This chapter, therefore, introduces the hardware devices that you must use—actually look at and touch—in order to interact with the computer and become part of the computer system.

Recall that, to become part of the computer system, you need a way to interact with the computer. That is what input devices—such as a keyboard, mouse, or touch screen—are used for. Similarly, the computer must be able to interact with you, so it relies on a set of hardware tools called output devices. These devices—such as the monitor, printer, or speakers—enable the computer to display the results of your work. Some types of devices, such as a modem, can perform both input and output functions.

The first part of this chapter is devoted to input devices, the second to output. The discussions focus on the hardware you will use most: the keyboard, mouse, monitor, and printer. You will learn what types of input and output devices are available and the advantages of each. At the end of the chapter, you will learn how ports, expansion cards, and expansion slots are used to connect I/O devices to the computer.

KEY CONCEPTS

The first step in learning to use a computer is becoming familiar with the components you will touch, look at, and interact with on a day-to-day basis. You need to get comfortable with the parts of the computer that enable you to input commands and data (the keyboard, mouse, and other types of input devices), and the parts that let the computer deliver information back to you (the monitor, printer, sound system, and other output devices).

The Keyboard

- The keyboard is the primary input device for entering text and numbers.
- There are five parts to the standard keyboard: the alphanumeric keys, the numeric keypad, the function keys, modifier keys, and the cursor movement keys.

The standard keyboard layout. ◄

Escape Key
Alphanumeric Keys
Function Keys

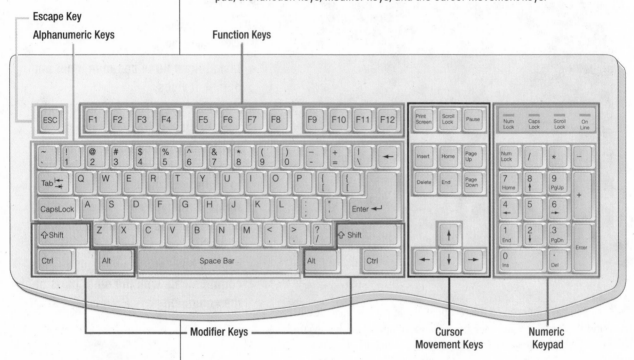

Modifier Keys — Cursor Movement Keys — Numeric Keypad

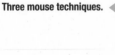

For information on **mice and other pointing devices**, visit this book's Web site at **www.glencoe.com/norton/online**

- When you press a key on a keyboard, the keyboard controller places the key's scan code in an area of memory called the keyboard buffer. When CPU time is available to accept the keystroke, the CPU receives it from the buffer.

The Mouse

- The mouse is a pointing device—an input device that lets you control the position of a graphical pointer on the screen without using the keyboard, and which enables you to issue commands and select options on screen without typing them at the keyboard.

Three mouse techniques. ◄

"click"

Click

"click click"

Double-click

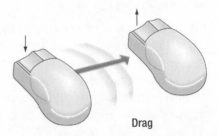

Drag

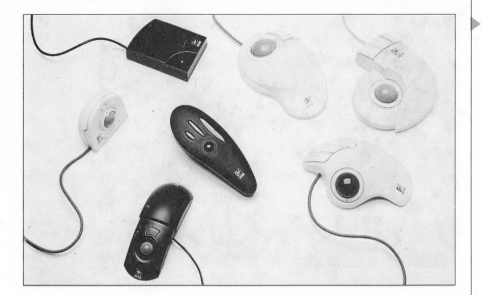

■ To use the mouse, you combine pointing with four techniques: clicking, double-clicking, dragging, and right-clicking.

■ Most mice operate with a ball that spins a set of rollers. If the mouse does not operate properly, you can clean it by removing the coverplate and ball and removing any debris, such as dust, from the ball and rollers.

■ A trackball provides the functionality of a mouse but requires less space on the desktop. Instead of moving the entire unit to roll the ball against the desktop, the unit sits still and you move the ball with your fingers.

■ A trackpad provides the functionality of a mouse but requires less space and less movement. You use a trackpad by dragging your finger across its touch-sensitive surface.

■ Some computers—especially newer notebook computers—feature a pointing device that is integrated into the keyboard. The device is a small joystick that sits between the G and H keys, and which can be maneuvered with one finger. This type of device is handy when there is no room for a mouse or trackball.

Other Input Devices

■ With pen-based computer systems, you use an electronic pen to write on a special pad or directly on the screen. In these systems, the pad or screen—not the pen—is the actual input device.

A handheld scanner.

- Touch-screen computers accept input directly through the monitor.

- Bar code readers, such as those used in grocery stores, can read bar codes, translate them into numbers, and input the numbers for the user.

- Image scanners convert printed images into digitized formats that can be stored and manipulated in computers.

- An image scanner equipped with optical character recognition (OCR) software can translate a page of text into a string of character codes in the computer's memory.

- Microphones can accept auditory input and turn it into text and computer commands with voice recognition (speech recognition) software.

- PC video cameras and digital cameras can digitize full-motion and still images, which can be stored and edited on the PC or transmitted over a LAN or the Internet.

The Monitor

- Computer monitors are roughly divided into two categories: cathode ray tube (CRT) and flat-panel monitors.

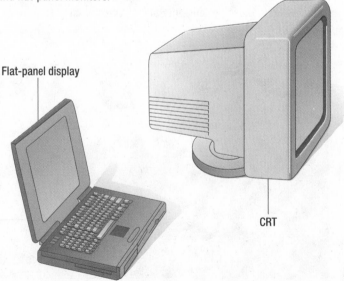

Flat-panel display

CRT

The two most common types of monitors.

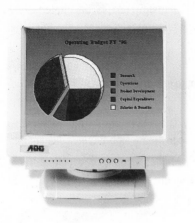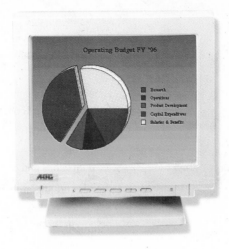

Comparison of a 17-inch monitor with a 15-inch monitor.

- A CRT monitor works with an electron gun that systematically aims a beam of electrons at every pixel on the screen.
- When purchasing a monitor, you must consider the size, resolution, refresh rate, and dot pitch.
- The video controller is an interface between the monitor and the CPU.
- Most flat-panel monitors are either active matrix or passive matrix (dual-scan).

Printers

- Ink jet and laser printers are the most commonly used printers in homes and business.
- When evaluating printers, you should consider image quality, speed, initial cost, and cost of operation.
- Ink jet printers work by spraying tiny droplets of ink onto the paper. Using sophisticated control mechanisms, these printers can create very detailed images in black and white or full color.
- Ink jet printers are inexpensive for both color and black printing, have low operating costs, and offer quality and speed comparable to low-end laser printers.

Ink jet technology is the basis for many new "all-in-one" office systems.

- Laser printers operate by bonding electrically charged particles of toner at precise points on the paper. To do this, the printer uses a complex system involving an electrostatic roller, light, heat, and finely powdered toner.

- Laser printers produce higher-quality print than ink jet printers and are fast and convenient to use, but they are also more expensive than ink jet printers.

- Thermal-wax, dye-sub, fiery, and IRIS printers are used primarily by print shops and publishers to create high-quality color images.

- Plotters create large-format images, usually for architectural or engineering uses, using mechanical drawing arms, ink jet technology, or thermal printing technology.

A laser printer produces its high-resolution output quickly and quietly.

Sound Systems

- Multimedia PCs generally come with sound systems, which include a sound card, speakers, and a microphone.

- The sound card translates digital signals into analog signals that drive the speakers.

For information on **installing expansion boards and other devices,** visit this book's Web site at **www.glencoe.com/norton/online**

Connecting I/O Devices to the Computer

- External devices—such as those used for input and output—are connected via ports on the back of the computer.

- Expansion slots on a PC's motherboard give external devices access to the computer's bus via expansion boards and provide I/O ports on the back of the computer.

- Most computers come with both serial and parallel ports.

- A small computer system interface (SCSI) port extends the bus outside the computer by way of a cable, which allows devices to be connected to one another in a daisy chain. In a daisy chain configuration, each new device is plugged into the device that precedes it, forming a chain of devices.

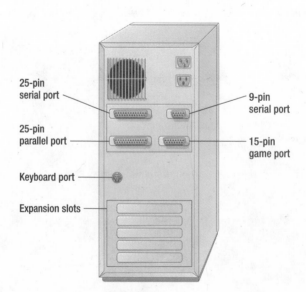

25-pin serial port

25-pin parallel port

Keyboard port

Expansion slots

9-pin serial port

15-pin game port

Standard ports on a PC.

HANDS On Activities

INPUT AND OUTPUT DEVICES

The Interactive Browser Edition introduces you to a wide range of input and output devices. As you work through Chapter 3 of the Interactive Browser Edition, you will learn about the most commonly used devices, as well as some alternative devices that are growing in popularity. You also will find demonstrations that show you how a monitor displays information, how printers print, and more.

The following sections are designed to help you navigate Chapter 3. As you work through the chapter, be sure to answer the review questions on the following pages. Write your answers directly in this book.

The Keyboard

The keyboard is the most commonly used input device. Many users spend hours a day at a computer keyboard, and they will tell you two things: first, it helps if you know how to type; second, you should find a keyboard that you are comfortable using, to reduce fatigue and the risk of stress injuries. As you will see, keyboards are taking many different shapes.

From the navigation menu on the left side of your browser window, choose The Keyboard. Use this menu item's options to explore this section of the chapter. As you work through this section, answer the following questions:

1. A computer keyboard features five groups of keys. Name them here:

_____ , _____ , _____ ,

_____ , and _____ .

2. What does the Esc key do?

_____

_____

_____

3. The most common keyboard layout used today has how many keys?

_____

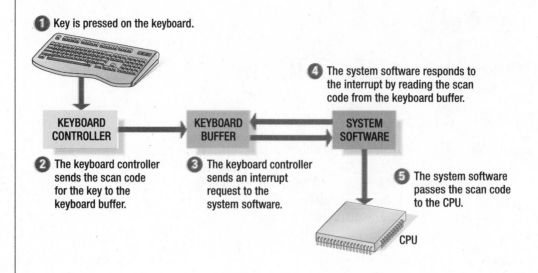

1 Key is pressed on the keyboard.

4 The system software responds to the interrupt by reading the scan code from the keyboard buffer.

KEYBOARD CONTROLLER

KEYBOARD BUFFER

SYSTEM SOFTWARE

2 The keyboard controller sends the scan code for the key to the keyboard buffer.

3 The keyboard controller sends an interrupt request to the system software.

5 The system software passes the scan code to the CPU.

CPU

4. What are the functions of the keyboard controller and the keyboard buffer?

_____

_____

_____

5. Why must the keyboard buffer be able to hold multiple keystrokes?

_____

_____

_____

From the set of options under The Keyboard, choose Self Check: Keyboard Input. Complete the quiz on screen; follow the instructions on the screen as you go.

The Mouse

It is hard to believe that many users once scoffed at the notion of using a mouse with a computer. But with the advent of graphical user interfaces, such as the Macintosh operating system, Windows, and some versions of UNIX, the mouse became an important input device because it enabled users to issue commands and choose options from menus and graphical toolbars instead of typing them. Today, some users—such as graphic artists and designers—rely more on the mouse than their keyboard.

From the navigation menu on the left side of your browser window, choose The Mouse. Use this menu item's options to explore this section of the chapter. As you work through this section, answer the following questions:

1. What is a pointer used for?

_____

_____

_____

_____

_____

_____

2. Why is the mouse credited with making computing more intuitive?

_____

_____

_____

_____

_____

_____

3. The four basic mouse techniques are:

_____,

_____,

_____, and

_____.

4. What is the difference between clicking and double-clicking?

_____

_____

_____

_____

_____

_____

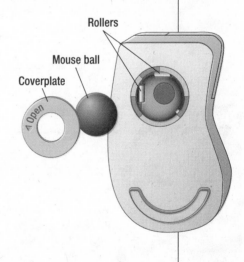

Rollers

Mouse ball

Coverplate

Open

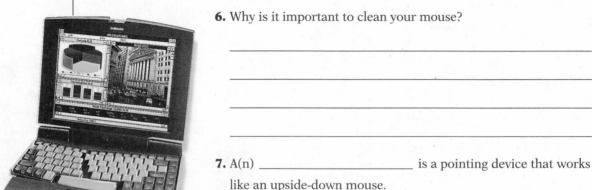

5. The most common type of mouse uses a(n) _____ and _____ to detect the mouse's motion.

6. Why is it important to clean your mouse?

_____

_____

_____

_____

7. A(n) _____ is a pointing device that works like an upside-down mouse.

8. Some computer keyboards—especially those used with laptop computers—now feature a(n) _____ or a(n) _____ rather than a mouse or trackball.

Productivity Tip

Now, review this chapter's Productivity Tip section, which discusses different options for entering commands and navigating documents. Of the methods described here, which one do you think will work best for you, and why?

_____

_____

_____

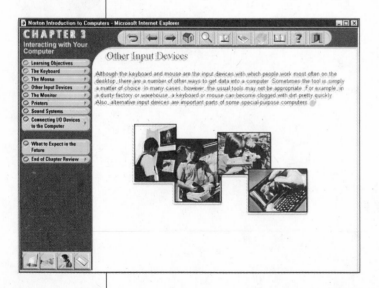

Other Input Devices

The keyboard and mouse are not the only input devices available for use with a computer. Many specialized input devices exist, each designed to accept a specific type of data for the computer to use. If you need to input audio or graphical data, for example, there is an input device for the job.

From the navigation menu on the left side of your browser window, choose Other Input Devices. Use this menu item's options to explore this section of the chapter. As you work through this section, answer the following questions:

1. In a pen-based system, which component acts as the input device?

_____

2. Give an example of a situation where a touch screen would be the most appropriate input device for a computer. Have you actually seen a touch screen used in the situation you describe?

_____

_____

_____

3. When you pass a bar code over a bar code reader, how does the reader know whether the image is upside down or not?

_____

_____

_____

4. A(n) _____ translates printed images into an electronic format that can be stored in a computer's memory.

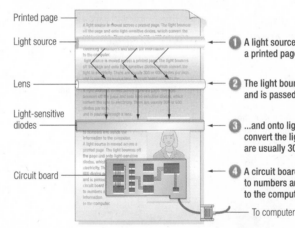

Printed page

Light source

Lens

Light-sensitive diodes

Circuit board

1 A light source is moved across a printed page.

2 The light bounces off the page and is passed through a lens...

3 ...and onto light-sensitive diodes, which convert the light to electricity. There are usually 300 or 600 diodes per inch.

4 A circuit board converts the electricity to numbers and sends the information to the computer.

To computer

5. In computers with fax modems, software called

_____

can convert faxes they receive directly into text that can be edited with a word processor.

6. How does one "train" speech recognition software? Why is it sometimes necessary to do so?

_____

_____

_____

_____

_____

7. PC video cameras _____ images by breaking them into individual pixels.

8. What does a video card enable the user to accomplish?

_____

_____

_____

9. A(n) _____ is a portable, handheld device that captures still images.

10. What does it mean to "digitize" an image or sound?

_____

_____

_____

The Monitor

If the keyboard is the most commonly used input device, then the monitor is the most commonly used output device. The monitor gives the user instant feedback about tasks being performed by the computer, whether showing a letter as it is being typed, or the progress of a message that is being faxed to another computer. Monitor technology has greatly improved in the last decade, making these devices sharper, more colorful, and less straining on the eyes. This section introduces the two most basic types of computer monitors and explains how they function.

From the navigation menu on the left side of your browser window, choose The Monitor. Use this menu item's options to explore this section of the chapter. As you work through this section, answer the following questions:

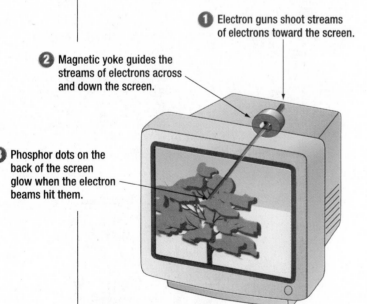

1 Electron guns shoot streams of electrons toward the screen.

2 Magnetic yoke guides the streams of electrons across and down the screen.

3 Phosphor dots on the back of the screen glow when the electron beams hit them.

1. The two basic types of monitors used with PCs are the

_____

and the

_____ .

2. Monitors display colors in three ways. Name and describe them.

_____

_____

_____

3. In a CRT monitor, what is a pixel?

_____

_____

_____

4. _____, _____, _____, and _____ are the most important specifications to check when purchasing a monitor.

5. How is a computer monitor's size measured? _____

_____

6. The _____ of a computer monitor is classified by the number of on the screen, expressed as a matrix.

7. The Video Graphics Array (VGA) standard resolution is _____ .

The Super VGA (SVGA) standard extended resolutions to _____ and _____ .

8. A monitor's _____ measures the distance between the phosphor dots that make up a single pixel. A measurement of _____ is considered the maximum you should accept.

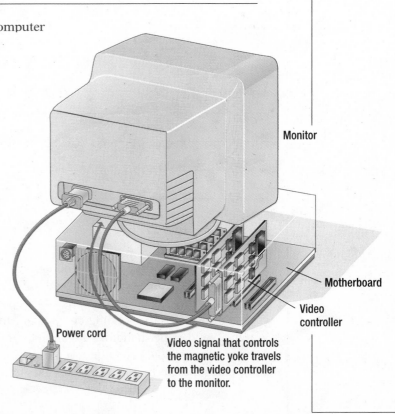

Monitor

Motherboard

Video controller

Power cord

Video signal that controls the magnetic yoke travels from the video controller to the monitor.

9. A(n) _____ is a circuit board that contains the video-dedicated memory and other circuitry necessary to send information to the monitor for display on the screen.

10. Video RAM (VRAM) is "dual-ported." What does that mean?

_____

_____

_____

11. What is the difference between an active matrix display and a passive matrix display?

_____

_____

_____

Now, review this chapter's Norton Notebook section, which discusses different methods for making Web pages accessible to persons with disabilities. After reading this section, find at least one Web site that you think would be difficult to use for someone with a disability. What would you do to improve the site's accessibility?

_____

_____

_____

_____

_____

_____

Printers

Printer technology has made tremendous progress in recent years. In the 1980s, when personal computers came into widespread use, the choice of printers was extremely limited. Most printers were slow and difficult to set up, and offered very few features. Today, however, literally thousands of different printers are available, offering a wide array of fonts, graphics, and paper-handling capabilities. Printers are categorized according to the method they use to create an image or text on the page. This section introduces each of those categories and explains the best uses for each.

From the navigation menu on the left side of your browser window, choose Printers. Use this menu item's options to explore this section of the chapter. As you work through this section, answer the following questions:

1. When evaluating printers, _____ , _____ , _____ , and _____ are the most important criteria to consider.

2. How does an ink jet printer create an image?

_____

_____

_____

_____

_____

3. How does a laser printer create an image?

_____

_____

_____

_____

_____

4. The most common laser printers print at a resolution of _____ , but high-end printers attain resolutions of up to _____ .

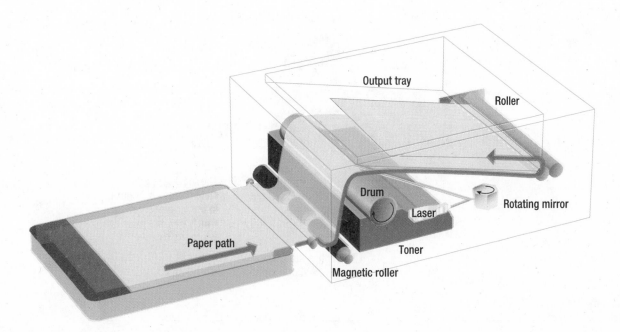

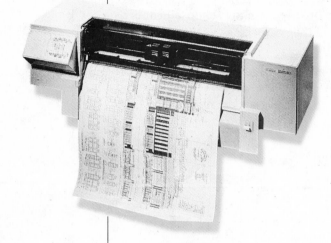

5. _____ printers provide vivid colors, because they use inks that do not bleed into each other or soak the specially coated paper.

6. A(n) _____ uses a robotic arm to draw with colored pens on oversized paper.

Sound Systems

Apart from the occasional beep, computers used to be silent machines. Today's computer systems are not only able to play sounds of all types, but work as full-fledged musical instruments. Specially equipped PCs provide many of the capabilities of a professional recording studio. Because users needed their systems to play multimedia products (such as games and electronic encyclopedias), computer makers began adding sound cards, speakers, and microphones to computers. These components, which once were considered strictly add-ons, are now standard features on nearly every new PC sold. This section discusses these components.

From the navigation menu on the left side of your browser window, choose Sound Systems. As you work through this section, answer the following questions:

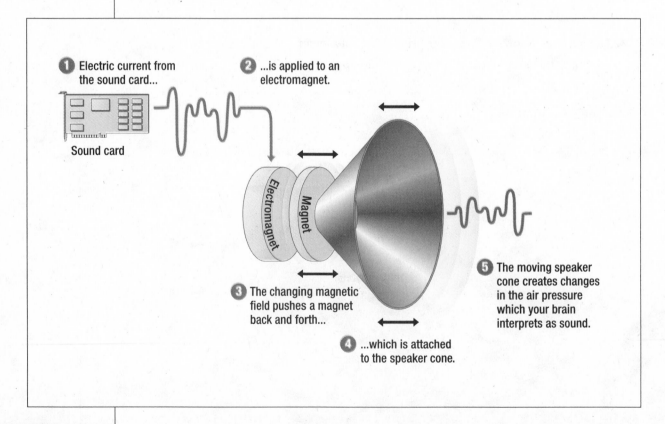

① Electric current from the sound card...

② ...is applied to an electromagnet.

Sound card

Electromagnet

Magnet

③ The changing magnetic field pushes a magnet back and forth...

④ ...which is attached to the speaker cone.

⑤ The moving speaker cone creates changes in the air pressure which your brain interprets as sound.

1. A(n) _____ is defined as being capable of producing high-quality text, graphics, animation, video, and sound.

2. A fully loaded multimedia PC may include the following five components:

_____ , _____ , _____ ,

_____ , and _____ .

Techview

Now, review this chapter's Techview section, which discusses the uses of sound in computers. What do you think would be the ultimate (most useful, entertaining, etc.) application for sound in a computer?

_____

_____

_____

_____

_____

_____

Connecting I/O Devices to the Computer

One reason for the PC's popularity (although the same is true of most types of computers) is the fact that you can add new components to it, or replace old components with updated ones. Generally, when you want to add a device to a computer, you "plug it into" one of the computer's ports or slots. Although this may sound intimidating, this expandability makes it relatively easy for many users to upgrade their computer. This section examines the different types of ports and expansions slots in a computer, and explains how you can use them to install new components.

From the navigation menu on the left side of your browser window, choose Connecting I/O Devices to the Computer. Use this menu item's options to explore this section of the chapter. As you work through this section, answer the following questions:

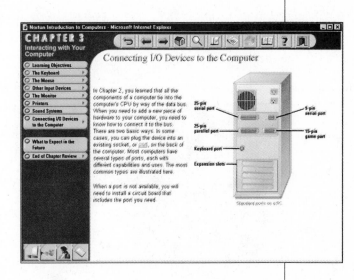

1. What are the two basic ways to add a new component to a computer?

_____

_____

_____

2. A(n) _____ is a channel through which 8 or more data bits can flow simultaneously.

3. A(n) _____ is a channel through which a single data bit can flow at one time.

4. Parallel ports are most frequently used to connect a(n) _____ to the computer, while serial ports are most frequently used to connect a(n) _____ or a(n) _____ .

5. A(n) _____ is an extension of the computer's bus, which provides a way to add new components to the computer.

6. What is an expansion board?

_____

_____

_____

_____

_____

_____

_____

_____

_____

_____

_____

_____

_____

_____

Parallel device (printer)

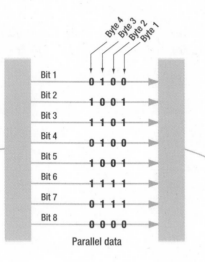

Byte 4 Byte 3 Byte 2 Byte 1

Bit 1   0 1 0 0
Bit 2   1 0 0 1
Bit 3   1 1 0 1
Bit 4   0 1 0 0
Bit 5   1 0 0 1
Bit 6   1 1 1 1
Bit 7   0 1 1 1
Bit 8   0 0 0 0

Parallel data

Computer

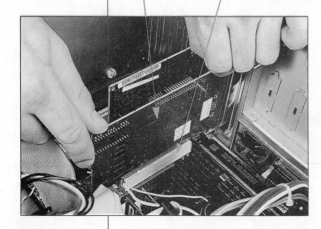

Expansion card

Expansion slot

7. List two purposes served by the expansion slots in a computer.

_____

_____

_____

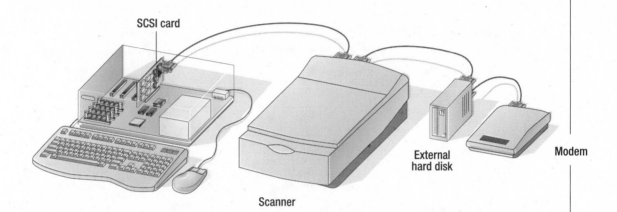

SCSI card

Scanner

External
hard disk

Modem

8. What does the acronym "SCSI" stand for? _____

9. What advantage does SCSI offer?

_____

_____

_____

From the set of options under Connecting I/O Devices to the Computer, choose Self Check: Serial and Parallel Interfaces. Complete the quiz on screen; follow the instructions on the screen as you go.

What to Expect in the Future

From the user's perspective, interacting with the computer is often the most frustrating part of using one. Although great strides have been made in computer interfaces, input devices, and output devices, users commonly encounter obstacles when trying to input data and commands, or when trying to get the system to produce the most pleasing output.

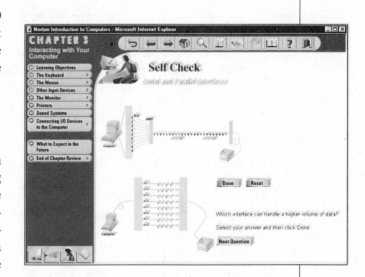

From the navigation menu on the left side of your browser window, choose What to Expect in the Future. Study the discussion and answer the following questions:

1. If you had the choice of keyboard input, voice input, or handwritten input, which method would you choose, and why?

_____

_____

_____

2. If computers are someday able to recognize speech (to accept commands and input), should they also be able to "talk back" to the user? If this technology existed, how would you like to see it used?

_____

_____

_____

3. Do you believe that computer technology will ever advance to the point that the "paperless office" becomes a reality? Why or why not?

_____

_____

_____

Computers
In Your Career

Now, review this chapter's Computers in Your Career section, which discusses the ways in which the technologies covered in this chapter could affect your career. In the space provided here, describe the area of technology that you think might most affect your career, and explain why:

_____

_____

_____

_____

_____

_____

_____

_____

End of Chapter Review

The End of Chapter Review section is designed to refresh you on the major points presented in this chapter, and to test your understanding of the information.

From the navigation menu on the left side of your browser window, choose End of Chapter Review. Use the menu item's options to review the Visual Summary sections for this chapter, review the chapter's Key Terms, and take the end-of-chapter quizzes.

VISUAL SUMMARIES

Review each of this chapter's Visual Summaries in turn. Each Visual Summary provides a quick overview of the major points in each section of the chapter. If you want more information about any item in a Visual Summary, click the link button next to that item, and you will return to the full discussion of that topic. (Then choose the Go Back button to return to the Visual Summary.)

KEY TERMS

Choose the Key Terms option if you need to find the definition for any of the important terms or concepts introduced in this chapter. To get a definition for a term, simply look up the term in the list and click it. The term's definition will appear in a separate window. Use this section to prepare yourself for the Key Term Quiz.

KEY TERM QUIZ

Complete the Key Term Quiz on your screen. You complete the quiz on screen, in crossword-puzzle form. When you are done with the test, choose the Solve button at the bottom of the screen. If you want to start over, choose the Reset button to clear your responses and then start again.

REVIEW QUESTIONS

Complete the Review Questions on your screen. You complete the quiz by typing correct responses in the blanks provided, selecting responses from a list, or by selecting option buttons. When you are done with the test, choose the Done button at the bottom of the screen. If you want to start over, choose the Reset button to clear your responses and then start again.

DISCUSSION QUESTIONS

Complete the Discussion Questions on your screen. You complete the quiz by typing your answers in the text boxes provided. When you are done with the test, you can print your answers and give them to your instructor. Your instructor may choose to discuss these questions in class.

*inter*NET Workshop

Do the exercises described in the Internet Workshop section. Write your findings in the spaces provided here.

1. List the Web sites you examined for accessibility. How did they rate? (Good? Fair? Poor?) For what reasons? How would you improve their accessibility?

_____

_____

_____

_____

_____

_____

2. How many audio-enabled Web sites did you find? List their names and URLs, note what type of content they offered (music, news, etc.), and whether you were required to install a plug-in before your browser could download the audio content.

_____

_____

_____

_____

_____

3. Note the names and URLs of the Web sites you found that offered product information and reviews for the following types of products:

■ Pointing devices: _____

_____

_____

_____

_____

■ Printers: _____

_____

_____

_____

_____

CHAPTER 4

Storing Information in a Computer

OBJECTIVES

When you complete this chapter, you will be able to do the following:

- List four common types of storage devices.
- Name three common uses of floppy disks.
- Name the four data disk areas on floppy and hard disks.
- List three ways tape drives differ from disk drives.
- Identify four types of optical storage devices.
- Name and describe the four main disk drive interface standards.

Up to this point, you have learned a great deal about the way computers process data and complete tasks with such incredible speed. But once all that data has been processed, where does it go? If ROM holds only the essential information that the computer needs to start up, and if RAM loses its contents when the machine is turned off, where do you store all those letters, spreadsheets, databases, and other information? And what about the operating system and other programs that are run on the computer? Where do you keep them?

The answer is simple: storage devices. Many different types of storage devices are used in computers, but they all serve the same purpose—to preserve and protect data and programs so that they are available whenever you need them. Storage media and devices have evolved dramatically since computers were in their infancy, and this pace has accelerated since the introduction of PCs. Some storage devices, such as magnetic disks and optical disks, enable you to load needed programs and data instantly. Others, such as tape, are meant for long-term storage, to preserve data that may not be needed for a long time.

This chapter introduces you to a wide variety of storage devices, and explains how you can use them to store and retrieve data and programs. You will get demonstrations showing how some storage devices work, and learn about the best uses for each kind of device.

NORTON
Online

For more
information on
storage devices, visit
this book's Web site at
www.glencoe.com/norton/online

KEY CONCEPTS

As you work with computers, you may come into contact with many types of data storage devices. In fact, many users find the variety of storage options to be mind-boggling. Each type of storage device is best suited for certain situations; selecting the right type of storage device depends on your understanding of the different technologies and their applications.

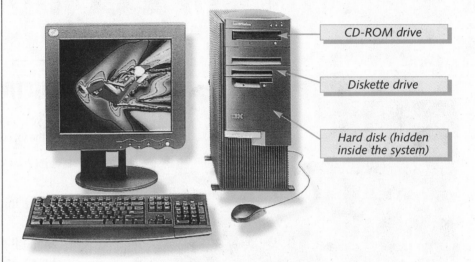

CD-ROM drive

Diskette drive

Hard disk (hidden inside the system)

Types of Storage Devices

- The materials on which data is stored are called storage media.

- The hardware components that read data from, or write data to, a storage medium are called storage devices.

- Storage devices can be classified as magnetic or optical.

- The most common magnetic storage devices are diskettes (also called floppy disks), hard disks, magnetic tape, and removable hard disks. These devices all use a magnetic storage medium—on the surface of a spinning disk or a tape—to store data, in much the same way a cassette tape stores music.

- The most common optical devices are compact disk read-only memory (CD-ROM), write once read many (WORM) disks, phase-change rewritable disks, magneto-optical disks, and floptical disks. These devices utilize lasers and special storage media to hold data.

Magnetic Storage Devices

- Magnetic storage devices work by polarizing tiny pieces of iron in the magnetic medium on the surface of a disk or tape.

- Read/write heads contain electromagnets that create magnetic fields on the medium. These heads can write data to the magnetic medium, and read data from the medium.

- Diskette drives, also known as floppy disk drives, write data to and read data from diskettes. Diskettes are also called floppy disks, or just floppies.

- Diskettes are most often used to transfer files between computers, as a means for distributing software, and as a backup medium.

You can make a magnet by wrapping a wire coil around an iron bar and sending an electric current through the coil. This produces an *electromagnet*.

IRON BAR

CURRENT

COPPER WIRE

If you reverse the direction of the current, the polarity of the magnet also reverses.

CURRENT

How an electromagnet creates a field on a magnetic surface.

If you place the electromagnet against a magnetic surface, such as the coating of a diskette...

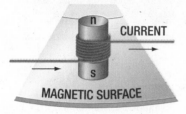

CURRENT

MAGNETIC SURFACE

...the electromagnet's pole induces an opposite field on the magnetic surface.

MAGNETIC SURFACE

- Diskettes come in two common sizes: 3.5-inch and 5.25-inch.

- Before a disk (diskette or hard disk) can be used, it must be formatted, or initialized—a process in which the read/write heads record tracks and sectors on the disk.

- The amount of data a disk can hold depends in large part on how it is formatted, as well as its physical size. Depending on how it is formatted, for example, a 3.5-inch diskette may be able to hold 720 KB, 800 KB, 1.44 KB, or 2.88 KB of data. A 5.25-inch disk, though physically larger, actually holds less data than a similarly formatted 3.5-inch disk—360 KB or 1.2 MB. Hard disks vary widely in size, from 40 MB to more than 10 GB.

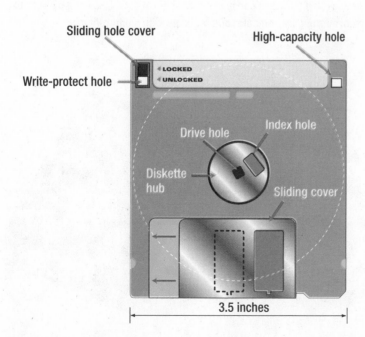

Sliding hole cover

High-capacity hole

Write-protect hole

LOCKED
UNLOCKED

Drive hole

Index hole

Diskette hub

Sliding cover

3.5 inches

3.5-inch diskette.

Distance between a hard disk's read/write head and the disk's surface, compared to the size of possible contaminants.

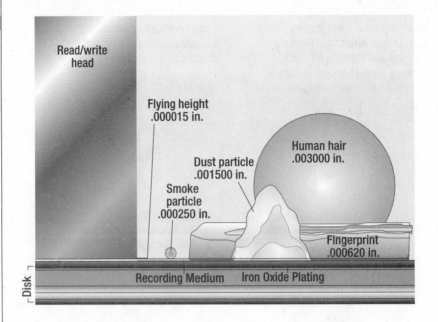

Read/write head

Flying height
.000015 in.

Dust particle
.001500 in.

Human hair
.003000 in.

Smoke particle
.000250 in.

Fingerprint
.000620 in.

Disk

Recording Medium   Iron Oxide Plating

- At the same time as the physical formatting is taking place, the computer's operating system in a PC establishes the disk's logical formatting by creating the boot sector, the file allocation table (FAT), the root folder, and the data area. These parts of the disk enable the computer to easily locate data that is stored on the disk, and find room to write new data to the disk.

- Hard disks can store more data than diskettes because the high-quality media, the high rotational speed, and the tiny distance between the read/write head and the disk surface permit densely packed data and rapid access.

- Hard disks also can store large quantities of data because they incorporate multiple disks—called platters—which are stacked inside the disk drive. In most hard drives, data can be stored on both sides of each platter, and each platter has its own read/write head.

- Removable hard disks combine high capacity with the convenience of diskettes. Like a hard disk, a removable hard disk can hold a great deal of data. Like a floppy disk, it can easily be removed from the computer and replaced with a different disk.

These two photos show the inside of a hard disk drive. The stack of platters is shown on the left. On the right is the circuitry that controls the drive. When they are installed in the computer, the circuitry is screwed to the top of the case that contains the hard disk.

This SyQuest SyJet drive records and reads data from small cartridges that can store up to 1.5 GB.

- The best removable hard disks are now as large and fast as good internal hard disks.

- Because data stored on magnetic tape is accessed sequentially, it is most appropriate for backup, when the cost and capacity of the medium are of concern, but speed is not.

Optical Storage Devices

- CD-ROM uses the same technology as a music CD does; a laser reads data from lands and pits in the disk's surface.

- CD-ROM disks can store 650 MB, but they cannot be written to.

- Digital Versatile Disk (DVD) technology may soon replace current CD-ROM technology in computers. DVD is a high-density medium that is capable of storing a full-length movie on a single disk the size of a CD—up to 9.4 GB. DVD drives can play current CD-ROM disks, as well as DVD disks.

- WORM disks and CD-Recordable disks can be written to once, but not rewritten or erased.

NORTON Online

For more information on **CD-ROM and DVD drives**, visit this book's Web site at **www.glencoe.com/norton/online**

You put a compact disk in a computer the same way you put one in your stereo.

- Phase-change rewritable drives enable you to write to a phase-change disk more than once.

- Magneto-optical drives write data with a high-powered laser, capable of melting the plastic on the disk coating, and a magnet that aligns the crystals under the melted area. A less powerful laser reads the alignment of the crystals.

Measuring Drive Performance

- When considering the performance of storage devices, you must know the average access time and the data-transfer rate.

- The average access time is the average time it takes a read/write head to move from one place on the recording medium to any other place on the medium.

- The data-transfer rate is a measure of how long it takes the device to read or write a given amount of data.

- The fastest access times and data-transfer rates are provided by hard disks, and some of the latest removable hard disks and magneto-optical disks. CD-ROMs have the slowest access times. Diskettes have the slowest data-transfer rates by far.

- A disk controller—the interface hardware between the CPU and the disk drive—usually conforms to one of three common interface standards: IDE, ESDI, or SCSI.

- IDE has been upgraded to Enhanced IDE. The upgraded interface standards support data-transfer rates as high as 16.6 MBps.

- SCSI, the second most common drive interface, essentially extends the capacity of the computer's bus.

- The most recent versions of SCSI support data-transfer rates from 10 to 40 MBps.

NORTON Online
For more information on **SCSI-2**, visit this book's Web site at **www.glencoe.com/norton/online**

HANDS On Activities

STORAGE TECHNOLOGIES AND HOW THEY WORK

The Interactive Browser Edition CD-ROM introduces you to a wide range of storage devices. As you work through Chapter 4 of the Interactive Browser Edition, you will learn about the most commonly used devices, as well as some new developments in storage technology that are gaining popularity. You also will find demonstrations that show you how a disk stores data, how disks are formatted, and more.

The following sections are designed to help you navigate Chapter 4. As you work through the chapter, be sure to answer the review questions on the following pages. Write your answers directly in this book.

Types of Storage Devices

Nearly all personal computers have at least two storage devices—a diskette drive and a hard drive—built into them, and it is now unusual to find a new PC that does not include a CD-ROM drive, as well. When you use the computer, these devices play an important role in your productivity and the security of your data. Still, your data storage and backup needs may be such that even more storage is required in your system. This section introduces the various types of storage devices available today, and describes some of the ways they are used.

From the navigation menu on the left side of your browser window, choose Types of Storage Devices. Use this menu item's options to explore this section of the chapter. As you work through this section, answer the following questions:

1. A(n) _____ is a flat piece of plastic, coated with iron oxide, and encased in a vinyl or plastic cover.

2. A(n) _____ consists of one or more rigid metal platters that are permanently encased in a drive.

3. _____ are defined as the physical components or materials on which data is stored.

4. A(n) _____ is defined as the hardware components that write data to, and read it from, storage media.

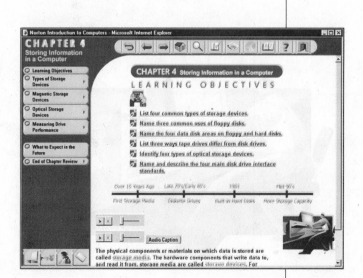

5. The two main categories of storage technologies are

_____ and _____ .

6. Describe the differences between diskettes and hard disks.

_____

_____

_____

7. Tape drives are typically used to _____ .

8. A(n) _____ uses the same technology as audio CD players.

Magnetic Storage Devices

The first storage devices in personal computers were magnetic. In the past decade, these devices have grown tremendously in capacity and speed, and remain the most popular storage option. Magnetic storage devices are interesting creations because they combine digital technology with recording technology that is decades old—the same processes used to record analog sounds on audio tape.

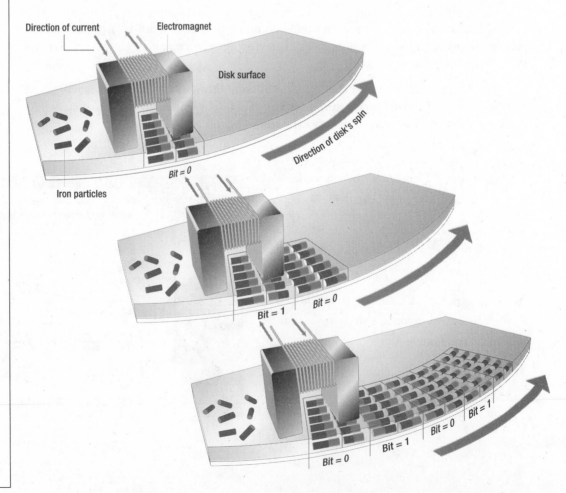

From the navigation menu on the left side of your browser window, choose Magnetic Storage Devices. Use this menu item's options to explore this section of the chapter. As you work through this section, answer the following questions:

1. A(n) _____ contains electromagnets that alter the polarity of magnetic particles on the storage medium.

2. Read/write heads record data as _____ .

3. The three most common uses for diskettes are:

_____

_____

_____

4. Why is it important to back up the files that are stored primarily on a hard disk?

_____

_____

_____

_____

1 If the read/write head needs to move from this sector...

...to this sector...

2 ...the drive spins the diskette all the way around and moves the read/write head all the way across the diskette's radius.

MOVE HEAD = 0.17 SEC

SPIN DISK = 0.2 SEC

The access time is the longer of the two operations — 0.2 sec.

5. What is access time, and why is it an important measure of a disk drive's performance?

_____

_____

_____

_____

6. The higher a diskette's _____ , the more data it can store.

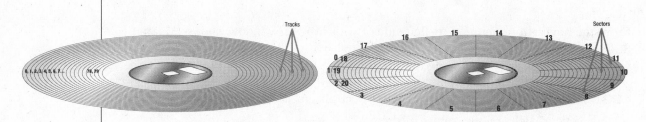

7. What does the formatting process do to a disk, and why is it necessary?

_____

_____

_____

_____

8. Is formatting required for both hard disks and diskettes? _____

9. What is the purpose of tracks and sectors on a formatted magnetic disk?

_____

_____

_____

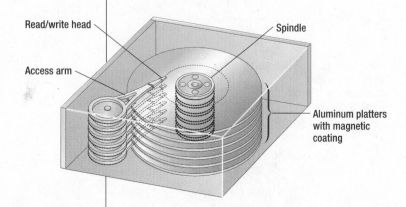

10. List three of the differences between diskette drives and hard drives.

_____

_____

_____

_____

_____

_____

11. In a formatted hard disk, the term _____ refers to the same track across all the disk sides.

12. What is special about a "hot swappable" hard disk?

_____

_____

_____

13. What is the primary difference between tape drives and hard disks?

_____

_____

_____

Productivity Tip

Now, review this chapter's Productivity Tip section, which discusses the importance of backing up your computer's files. Consider the way you use a computer—whether for fun, schoolwork, or business—and describe the primary threat that exists to your data files. Then, list the type of backup medium and backup procedure that would work best for you.

_____

_____

_____

_____

Optical Storage Devices

Optical storage devices started becoming popular among PC users in the early 1990s. Because of their large capacities (a compact disk can hold an entire encyclopedia, complete with sounds, animations, and more), optical disks quickly became accepted as a convenient way to distribute programs and large collections of data. Optical storage devices, however, also have two drawbacks. First, their access time tends to be slower than that of large-capacity hard disks. Second, data can be written onto most optical disks only once; after that, the data on the disk cannot be altered.

Thanks to recent advances in optical storage technology, however, and now that scientists are combining optical and magnetic technologies, those drawbacks are becoming minimized. Access times are continually improving, and some optical devices enable you to write data to the storage medium multiple times. New lower-cost technology allows users to "cut" their own compact disks at home. In fact, many industry observers feel confident that optical technology will replace magnetic technology as the basis for computer storage within the next decade.

From the navigation menu on the left side of your browser window, choose Optical Storage Devices. Use this menu item's options to explore this section of the chapter. As you work through this section, answer the following questions:

1. The two most commonly used optical storage technologies are

_____ and

_____ .

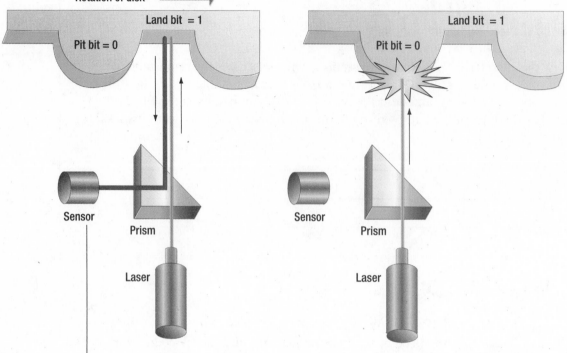

2. CD-ROM technology uses a(n) _____ to read data from the surface of a disk. On the disk, when the light strikes a(n) _____, it is reflected back to a sensor. When the light strikes a(n) _____, it is scattered.

3. A(n) _____ is just like a standard compact disk, but can hold much more data because it uses both sides of the disk.

4. You can attach a(n) _____ to your computer as a regular peripheral device, and use it to create your own compact disks.

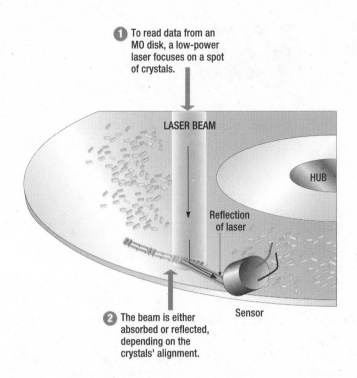

1 To read data from an MO disk, a low-power laser focuses on a spot of crystals.

LASER BEAM

HUB

Reflection of laser

Sensor

2 The beam is either absorbed or reflected, depending on the crystals' alignment.

5. You can use a(n) _____ system to store photographs.

6. What is the primary advantage of phase-change technology over standard CD technology?

_____

_____

_____

7. How does a magneto-optical drive write data to a disk?

_____

_____

_____

8. In a magneto-optical drive, the laser used to read data from a disk is _____ than the laser used to write data to the disk.

From the set of options under Optical Storage Devices, choose Self Check: Storage Device Technology. Complete the quiz on screen; follow the instructions on the screen as you go.

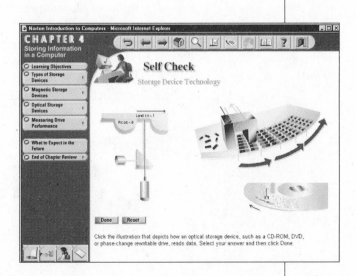

Techview

Now, review this
chapter's Techview
section, which discusses PC card technologies and their uses. What other potential
uses for PC card technology can you imagine, that aren't described in this discussion?
List them here.

_____

_____

_____

Measuring Drive Performance

Although data storage technologies are improving overall, remember that not all storage devices are created equal. Some have larger capacities, some can locate data faster, and some can transfer data from the medium to the CPU in less time. When selecting a storage device for your system, you need to evaluate these factors—as well as cost and compatibility. This section shows you how to measure the performance of most types of storage devices.

From the navigation menu on the left side of your browser window, choose Measuring Drive Performance. Use this menu item's options to explore this section of the chapter. As you work through this section, answer the following questions:

1. When evaluating the performance of common storage devices, you need to be aware of _____ and _____ .

2. Average access time for diskette drives is _____ . Average access time for most hard drives ranges from _____ to _____ .

3. What is the purpose of file compression, and why would you want to use it?

_____

_____

_____

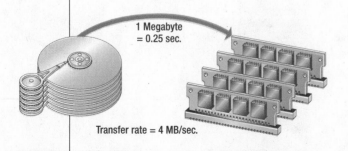

1 Megabyte
= 0.25 sec.

Transfer rate = 4 MB/sec.

4. Data-transfer rate is defined as _____ .

5. MBps stands for _____ ; Mbps stands for _____ .

Table 4.1	Average Access Times and Data-Transfer Rates for Common Storage Devices				
	HARD DISKS	REMOVABLE HARD DISKS	MAGNETO-OPTICAL	DISKETTES	CD-ROMS
Avg. Access Time (ms)	8–12	12–30	15–20	100	100–300
Data-Transfer Rate (MBps)	5–15	1.25–5.5	2–6	0.045	0.3–0.9

6. A disk controller performs what function?

_____

_____

_____

From the set of options under Measuring Drive Performance, choose Self Check: Storage Device Performance. Complete the quiz on screen; follow the instructions as you go.

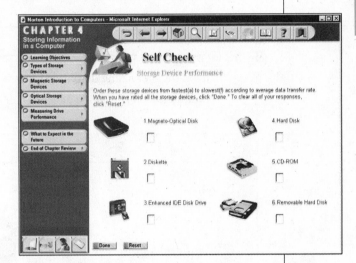

NORTON *Notebook*

Now, review this chapter's Norton Notebook section, which discusses data warehousing and data mining. List two types of businesses or organizations (other than those described in this discussion) that could make use of this technology, and explain how you think they could benefit from data warehousing and data mining.

1. _____

_____

2. _____

_____

What to Expect in the Future

In the world of data storage, the old adage "more is better" is like a rallying cry. PCs now commonly feature hard drives larger than 4 GB, built-in Zip drives, tape backup units, DVD drives, and other high-capacity storage devices. Everyone from home computer users to the giants of industry want more storage capacity and faster access times at lower cost. These demands are pushing data storage technology into new directions, away from magnetic storage and toward optics and even more futuristic devices.

From the navigation menu on the left side of your browser window, choose What to Expect in the Future. Study the discussion and answer the following questions:

1. Do you think it will ever be necessary for personal computers to feature storage devices that provide truly mass storage capabilities—for example, more than 100 GB? Why or why not?

_____

_____

_____

2. Given the increasing demands for storage capacity, do you think diskless network computers will gain wide acceptance? Why or why not?

_____

_____

_____

Computers
In Your Career

Now, review this chapter's Computers in Your Career section, which discusses the ways in which the technologies covered in this chapter could affect your career. In the space provided here, describe the area of technology that you think might most affect your career, and explain why:

_____

_____

_____

_____

_____

_____

End of Chapter Review

The End of Chapter Review section is designed to refresh you on the major points presented in this chapter, and to test your understanding of the information.

From the navigation menu on the left side of your browser window, choose End of Chapter Review. Use the menu item's options to review the Visual Summary sections for this chapter, review the chapter's Key Terms, and take the end-of-chapter quizzes.

VISUAL SUMMARIES

Review each of this chapter's Visual Summaries in turn. Each Visual Summary provides a quick overview of the major points in each section of the chapter. If you want more information about any item in a Visual Summary, click the link button next to that item, and you will return to the full discussion of that topic. (Then choose the Go Back button to return to the Visual Summary.)

KEY TERMS

Choose the Key Terms option if you need to find the definition for any of the important terms or concepts introduced in this chapter. To get a definition for a term, simply look up the term in the list and click it. The term's definition will appear in a separate window. Use this section to prepare yourself for the Key Term Quiz.

KEY TERM QUIZ

Complete the Key Term Quiz on your screen. You complete the quiz on screen, in crossword-puzzle form. When you are done with the test, choose the Solve button at the bottom of the screen. If you want to start over, choose the Reset button to clear your responses and then start again.

REVIEW QUESTIONS

Complete the Review Questions on your screen. You complete the quiz by typing correct responses in the blanks provided, selecting responses from a list, or by selecting option buttons. When you are done with the test, choose the Done button at the bottom of the screen. If you want to start over, choose the Reset button to clear your responses and then start again.

DISCUSSION QUESTIONS

Complete the Discussion Questions on your screen. You complete the quiz by typing your answers in the text boxes provided. When you are done with the test, you can print your answers and give them to your instructor. Your instructor may choose to discuss these questions in class.

*inter*NET Workshop

Do the exercises described in the Internet Workshop section. Write your findings in the spaces provided here.

1. How many companies did you find on the Web that provide backup services? List the URLs of the sites here, along with a brief summary of the services they provide.

_____

_____

_____

_____

2. Did you find any Web sites of companies that offer data-compression utilities? List each company's name and URL, along with the name of its compression product.

_____

_____

_____

3. List the names and URLs of Web sites you can find that sell the following devices:

■ Hard drives: _____

_____

_____

■ Removable hard drives: _____

_____

_____

■ DVD drives: _____

_____

_____

■ CD-ROM drives: _____

_____

_____

■ CD-R drives: _____

_____

_____

Assignment Record

Instructor _____ **Office Number** _____

Office Hours _____

Phone _____ **E-Mail** _____

Midterm Date _____ **Final Date** _____

	ASSIGNMENT DUE	SCORE	QUIZ DATE	SCORE	TEST DATE	SCORE
CHAPTER 1						
CHAPTER 2						
CHAPTER 3						
CHAPTER 4						
PART 1 QUIZ						
PART 1 TEST						

USING MICROCOMPUTER SOFTWARE

PART 2   USING MICROCOMPUTER SOFTWARE

CHAPTER **5**

The Operating System and the User Interface

The previous chapters have given you an in-depth look at computer systems overall and hardware components in particular. Now it is time to start learning about the part of the computer system that makes things work—software, especially operating system (OS) software.

Without an operating system, a computer is basically a worthless piece of hardware. The operating system provides the instructions that tell the computer what to do, manages its hardware components, and displays an interface for the user. Because the operating system plays such a critical role in the computer system, it is the first software to be installed on the computer, and usually is the first piece of software the new user learns to use.

This chapter introduces you to a number of operating systems. You will learn what the OS does for you and the background role it plays for other programs and hardware. You will look at the evolution of operating systems from Microsoft, the operating systems leader. Then you will review some of the other players in the operating systems game: IBM's OS/2 Warp, Apple Computer's Macintosh operating system, and UNIX. You will also see how operating systems are used to manage files, load programs, share data, and perform multitasking operations.

OBJECTIVES

When you complete this chapter, you will be able to do the following:

- Define the terms "operating system" and "user interface."
- Name three major functions of the operating system and explain the importance of each function from the user's perspective.
- List five types of utility software and describe how each can be used to enhance the functionality of an operating system.
- Define the term "multitasking" and list two ways it saves time for a user.
- Name at least three improvements that Windows offers over DOS.
- List three other significant operating systems, aside from DOS and Windows.

KEY CONCEPTS

No matter what you do with a computer, the operating system is involved. In fact, without the operating system, you would have no way of issuing commands to the computer or performing tasks such as printing or dialing a modem. This is because the operating system accepts your commands and translates them into instructions that the computer can understand. To get the most functionality from an operating system, you need to understand the many tasks it performs. The following sections provide an overview of operating systems and describe their responsibilities.

What Is an Operating System?

- The operating system is software, but is different from software programs such as word processors or spreadsheets. The operating system acts as the computer's master control program.

- When you turn on a computer, it loads the operating system, which assumes control of the system until the computer is turned off.

- The operating system provides a user interface, which enables the user to interact with the hardware and software programs.

- The operating system loads other software programs into memory so you can use them.

- The operating system manages the way programs interact with all the system's hardware components and other software.

- The operating system manages the way files are stored and retrieved on disks.

- By installing utility software on the computer, you can extend the operating system's functionality.

The User Interface

- Most modern operating systems employ a graphical user interface (GUI), which enables you to control the system by clicking on-screen graphics.

- A GUI is based on the desktop metaphor, in which the operating system acts as a surface on which various tools (programs, files, hardware devices, and other tools) reside. You can use any tool simply by choosing it from the desktop.

  - In a GUI, you can choose a command, file, device, or program by choosing its icon—a small graphic that represents a specific object in the system.

  - Most GUIs feature sizable windows, which display programs and documents.

  - When working in a GUI, you can issue commands by choosing them from menus, toolbars, and dialog boxes.

  - The applications designed to run under a particular operating system use the same interface elements, so you see a familiar interface no matter what you are doing on the computer.

The screen you see when you start Windows 98.

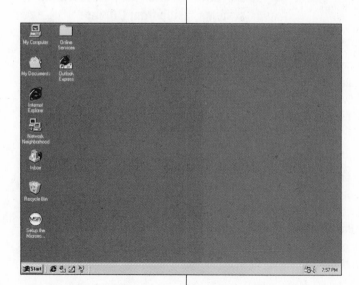

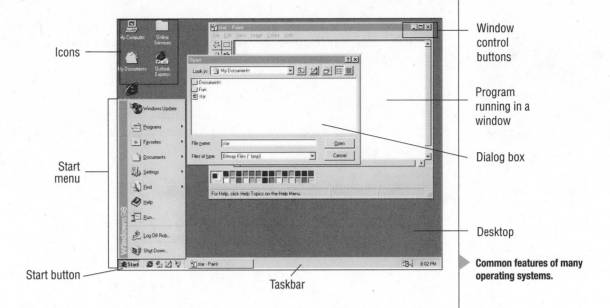

Icons

Start menu

Start button

Taskbar

Window control buttons

Program running in a window

Dialog box

Desktop

■ Some older operating systems, such as DOS, use command-line interfaces, which the user controls by typing commands at a prompt.

```
C:\>ver

Windows 95. [Version 4.00.950]
```

Running Programs

■ The operating system manages all the programs that are running on the computer, providing an interface between the program and the user, as well as an interface between the program and the hardware.

■ The operating system provides system-level services to programs, including file management (such as opening a document for editing), memory management (ensuring that the program has adequate memory space), and printing.

■ The operating system allows programs to share information. This capability enables you to copy or cut data from a document in one program and reuse it in another document or another program.

■ In Windows 3.1, 3.11, NT, 95, and 98, sharing is accomplished through a disk area called the Clipboard and a process called Object Linking and Embedding (OLE).

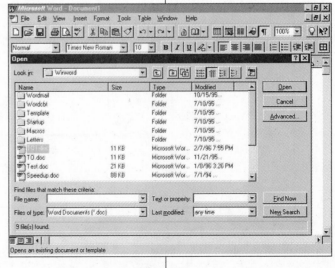

■ A modern operating system also makes multitasking possible. Multitasking is the ability to perform two or more procedures (such as printing a document while connecting to the Internet) simultaneously.

Managing Files

■ The operating system keeps track of all the program and data files—which can number in the hundreds—on each disk.

The My Computer window, showing the contents of a disk.

A hierarchical file system.

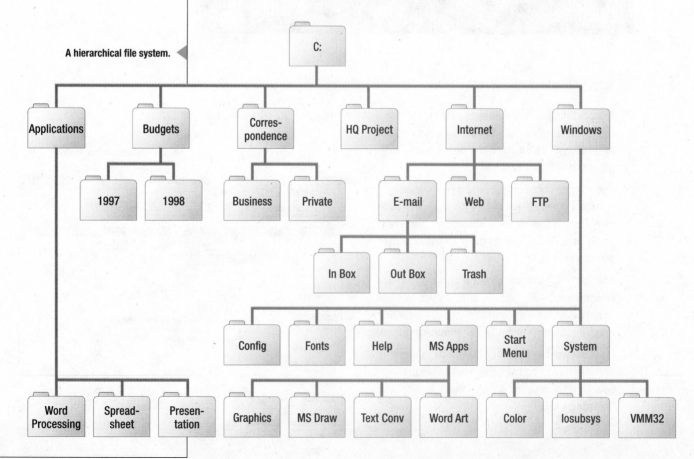

- On a PC, Windows tracks the location of files by constantly updating the file allocation table (FAT), which is a list of the disk's contents. The FAT is stored on the disk itself.

- Users can make their own file management easier by creating a hierarchical file system that includes folders and subfolders.

Managing Hardware

- The operating system uses interrupt requests (IRQs) to maintain organized communication with the CPU and the other pieces of hardware.

- Each of the hardware devices is controlled by another piece of software, called a driver, which allows the operating system to activate and use the device.

- The operating system also provides the software necessary to link computers and form a network.

Enhancing the Operating System with Utility Software

- Utility programs can be installed on a computer to enhance the functionality of the operating system, by performing tasks that the operating system cannot perform, or to actually replace a portion of the operating system.

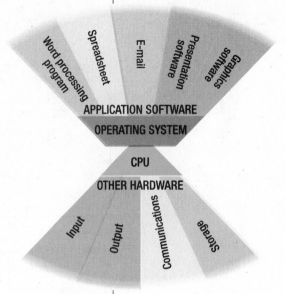

The operating system acts as an intermediary between the application software and all the hardware.

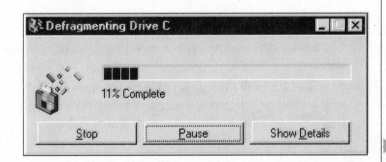

This dialog box shows the progress being made by the Disk Defragmenter utility as it defragments the files on the hard disk.

- As operating systems have evolved to perform a wider variety of tasks, some types of utilities have become unnecessary.

- The most common utilities are for file defragmentation, data compression, backup, data recovery, protection against viruses, and screen saving.

- File defragmentation utilities ensure that each file is stored as a whole and not broken into parts on the disk. This saves disk space and enables the computer to load files faster.

- Data compression utilities abbreviate sequences of bits, to make files as small as possible, so they require less disk space.

- Backup software helps users copy large groups of files from a hard disk to another storage medium. Backups help protect valuable data and conserve disk space.

- Data recovery software is used to recover data that has been mistakenly erased or somehow rendered unusable.

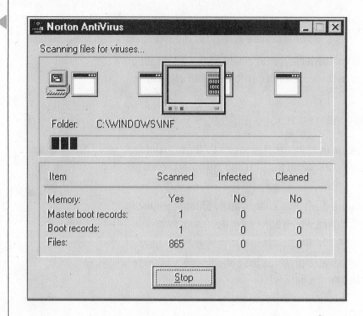

Antivirus utilities look at the boot sector and every executable file on a disk, and report how many are infected with viruses.

■ Antivirus utilities can scan disks and memory for viruses, which are parasitic programs that can damage or erase disk files. After finding a virus in a computer system, the antivirus utility can help the user eradicate the virus, and sometimes even reconstruct damaged files.

■ Screen savers display moving images on the screen, if the computer receives no input within a designated amount of time. Originally developed to protect monitors, screen savers now are used primarily for fun.

Microsoft Operating Systems

NORTON Online

For information on **all versions of Windows**, visit this book's Web site at www.glencoe.com/norton/online

■ DOS dominated the operating system market during the 1980s, but gradually became obsolete.

■ Windows 3.0, 3.1, and 3.11 provided a GUI for computers running DOS. They are operating environments, not true operating systems, and run on top of DOS.

The interface for Windows 3.0 and 3.1 has a lot in common with that of the Mac and Windows 95/98. Users work with files and programs by clicking desktop icons to open windows.

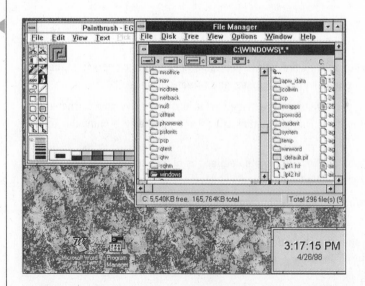

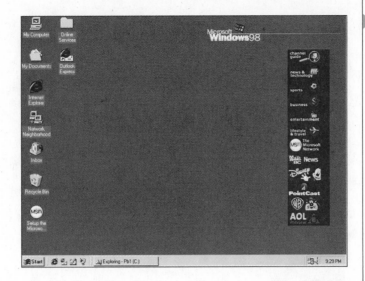

- The strengths of Windows 95 are its simplified interface, 32-bit processing, preemptive multitasking, and its ability to run older Windows and DOS programs. Unlike earlier versions of Windows, Windows 95 is a true operating system.

- Windows 98 is the latest upgrade to Windows 95. Its refinements include improved usability features, better speed and reliability, and new Internet-related capabilities.

- Microsoft Windows NT offers true 32-bit architecture and excellent networking capabilities. Two basic versions of Windows NT are available: Windows NT Server, which is a network operating system; and Windows NT Workstation, which is designed for use on desktop systems but also features networking capabilities.

- Windows CE brings many of the capabilities of Windows 95 to consumer electronics devices, such as personal digital assistants (PDAs). Microsoft hopes that Windows CE will become the OS of choice for all electronic devices that require or can accept programming or input, such as televisions, VCRs, microwave ovens, alarm systems, and more.

Windows CE is designed to run on many kinds of smaller computerized devices, such as handheld computers, PDAs, and others.

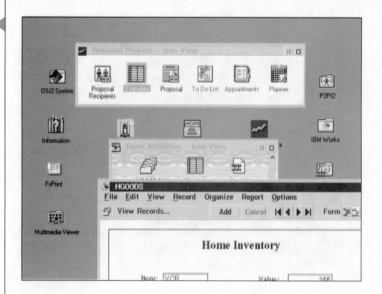

NORTON
Online

For information
on **these operating**
systems, visit this
book's Web site at
www.glencoe.com/norton/online

Other Operating Systems for Personal Computers

■ Although Microsoft has become the unquestioned market leader in operating systems, that has not always been the case. Other operating systems have been popular; and some continue to keep their staunch supporters' loyalty.

■ The Macintosh has long been a favorite among GUI fans, as well as publishers, multi-media developers, graphic artists, and schools, primarily because of its consistent interface, built-in networking, and plug-and-play hardware capability.

■ IBM's operating system is OS/2 Warp, a single-user, multitasking system for Intel-based machines.

■ UNIX was the first multiuser, multiprocessing operating system on personal computers, but it has been losing market share. UNIX, however, runs on many other types of computer systems, including supercomputers, mainframes, and minicomputers, and still has a strong user base in those markets.

HANDS On Activities

INPUT AND OUTPUT DEVICES

The Interactive Browser Edition introduces you to a variety of operating systems and explains their many functions. As you work through Chapter 5 of the Interactive Browser Edition, you will learn about the most popular operating systems and their differences. You also will find demonstrations that show you how an operating system manages data flow and hardware.

The following sections are designed to help you navigate Chapter 5. As you work through the chapter, be sure to answer the review questions on the following pages. Write your answers directly in this book.

What is an Operating System?

Because it acts as the computer's master control program, the operating system's importance is hard to overstate. The more you know about your PC's operating system, the more functionality you can get from your system, and the more productive your computer use will be. This section introduces you to the OS and its many duties; after you read this section, you will understand why operating systems are so crucial.

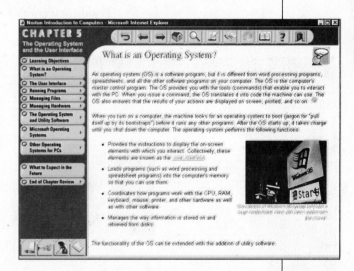

From the navigation menu on the left side of your browser window, choose What Is an Operating System? Use this menu item's options to explore this section of the chapter. As you work through this section, answer the following questions:

1. When you issue a command, what does the operating system do with it?

_____

_____

_____

2. When you turn on a computer, the machine looks for an operating system to _____ before it runs any other programs.

3. The operating system performs four critical functions. What are they?

_____

_____

_____

_____

_____

_____

The User Interface

For years, developers made operating systems increasingly powerful and feature-rich, but paid little attention to their "user friendliness." The fact is, the more powerful an OS is, the easier it should be for people to use. With the advent of windowed operating systems, simplicity became a primary concern of developers, who had learned that users won't use features if they cannot find them or remember commands.

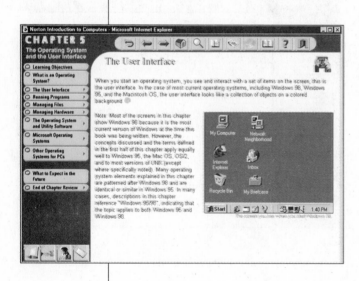

From the navigation menu on the left side of your browser window, choose The User Interface. Use this menu item's options to explore this section of the chapter. As you work through this section, answer the following questions:

1. The interface provided by a Windows-based computer (or a Macintosh or OS/2 system) is referred to as a(n) _____, because you point to graphics on the screen.

2. In a graphical user interface, images called _____ represent the parts of the computer you work with.

3. What happens when you double-click an icon on your operating system desktop?

_____

_____

_____

4. When you right-click many of the items on the Windows 95/98 desktop, what happens?

_____

_____

_____

5. When you start a program in Windows 95/98, a(n) _____
for it appears on the _____ .

6. In Windows 95/98, how do you open the Start menu, and what does it
enable you to do?

_____

_____

_____

7. In Windows 95/98, you can have more than one program running at one
time, but only one program can be active. How do you switch from one
program to another?

_____

_____

_____

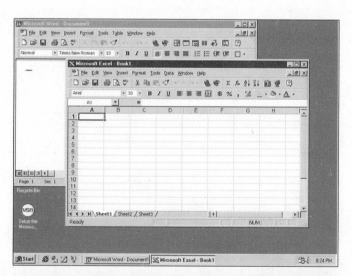

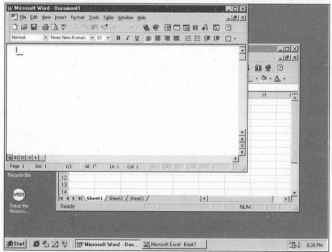

Chapter 5
Hands-On Activities

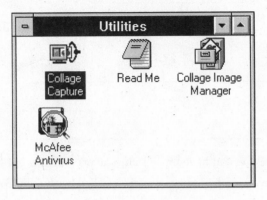

8. Each open application runs in a(n) _____ .

9. What do window control buttons enable you to do?

_____

_____

_____

_____

_____

_____

_____

_____

_____

10. Within a program, you can start tasks by choosing commands from lists, which are

called _____ .

11. Name three tools that you might nd in a typical dialog box.

_____

_____

_____

_____

_____

_____

_____

_____

12. A well-designed GUI offers consistency
and familiarity for the user, because:

_____

_____

_____

_____

_____

_____

13. The acronym DOS stands for

_____ .

From the set of options under The User Interface, choose Self Check: Identify the Parts of the Interface. Complete the quiz on screen; follow the instructions as you go.

Productivity Tip

Now, review this chapter's Productivity Tip section, which discusses the process of upgrading to a newer version of an operating system. Based on the description provided here, do you think there is an advantage to keeping the latest operating system on your computer? Do you think you could perform such an upgrade yourself?

_____

_____

_____

Running Programs

Just as you need the operating system in order to interact with the computer, so do application programs. The operating system acts as an intermediary between software programs and the computer, and between software programs and the user. Suppose, for example, that you are using a word processing program, and you want to open a le stored on disk. You issue the Open command in the program, which in turn issues a command to the operating system. This chain of command is required because the operating system actually controls the storage and retrieval of les.

From the navigation menu on the left side of your browser window, choose Running Programs. Use this menu item s options to explore this section of the chapter. As you work through this section, answer the following questions:

1. Software programs use instructions known as _____ to request services from the operating system.

2. Name four of the services that an operating system provides to programs:

_____

_____

_____

_____

3. What is the Clipboard, which is featured in many operating systems?

_____

_____

_____

4. What can you do by using the Cut, Copy, and Paste commands as illustrated on the next page?

_____

_____

_____

5. What special feature is provided when you use Object Linking and Embedding to share information between two different documents?

_____

_____

_____

_____

_____

_____

6. _____ is the ability to perform two or more procedures at the same time.

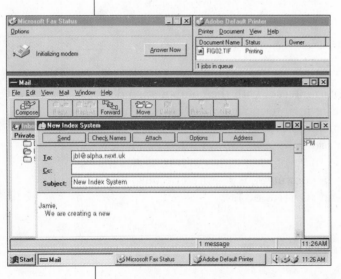

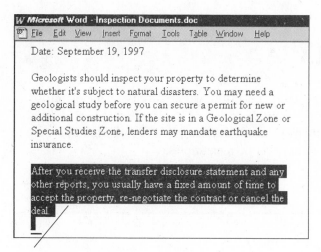

1. Select the text you want to move.

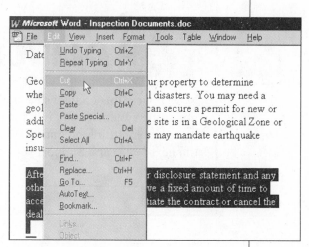

2. Use the Cut command to remove the selected text and place it in the Clipboard.

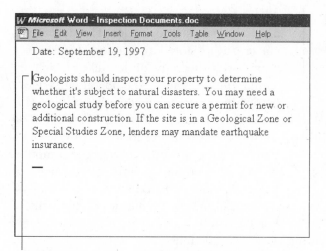

3. Move the insertion point to the text s new position in the document.

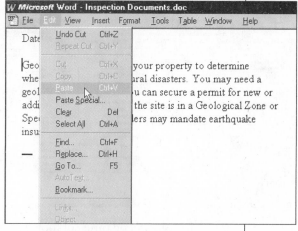

4. Use the Paste command to copy the text from the Clipboard to the new position in the document.

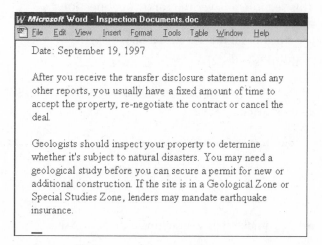

5. The moved text. A copy of the text remains in the Clipboard until the next time you use the Cut or Copy command.

Now, review this chapter's Norton Notebook section, which discusses the evolution of operating systems. Look into the future and describe the kinds of features and capabilities that you think operating systems will need (that is, will be demanded by users) in the next few years. Support your predictions with examples.

_____

_____

_____

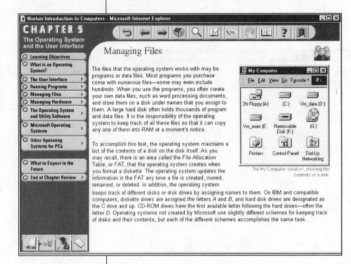

Managing Files

As you learned in previous chapters, all data in a computer is stored in files. The documents you create are stored as files, and software programs are collections of files, all of which are stored on disk. One of the operating system's many functions is to manage all those files. This involves knowing the location of every file on the disk and being able to access any file when it is needed by any other part of the computer system. An operating system's file-management capabilities affect the performance of the system overall, and greatly affect your productivity. For these reasons, modern operating systems feature a wide range of tools for working with files of all kinds.

From the navigation menu on the left side of your browser window, choose Managing Files. Use this menu item's options to explore this section of the chapter. As you work through this section, answer the following questions:

1. To keep track of all the files stored on a disk, the operating system maintains a list of files. This list is called the _____ .

2. How does the operating system distinguish among the different drives that are attached to the computer?

_____

_____

_____

3. To find files quickly, you can organize them by using _____ .

4. In Windows 95/98, there are two different programs for viewing and managing the

contents of a disk. These programs are
named _____ and

_____ .

5. In a(n) _____ , you
can organize multiple folders by placing
folders inside other folders.

Managing Hardware

When you issue the Print command in your
favorite software program, you are actually
issuing an operating system command. In fact,
any time you or a software program interacts
with a piece of hardware, the OS must be involved. This is because the operating system
controls the flow of data and instructions throughout the
system, to ensure that no con icting instructions or requests
are made at the same time. In its role as hardware manager,
therefore, the OS makes sure that things run smoothly.

Folders in the C: drive

Files   File   File   Date and time when
sizes   types   the le was last saved

From the navigation menu on the left side of your browser window, choose Managing
Hardware. Use this menu item s options to explore this section of the chapter. As you
work through this section, answer the following questions:

1. If the operating system did not coordinate all the hardware functions, what might happen?

_____

_____

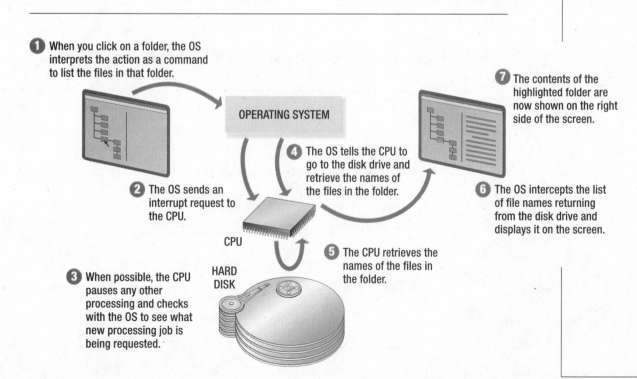

1 When you click on a folder, the OS interprets the action as a command to list the files in that folder.

7 The contents of the highlighted folder are now shown on the right side of the screen.

OPERATING SYSTEM

4 The OS tells the CPU to go to the disk drive and retrieve the names of the files in the folder.

2 The OS sends an interrupt request to the CPU.

6 The OS intercepts the list of file names returning from the disk drive and displays it on the screen.

CPU

5 The CPU retrieves the names of the files in the folder.

3 When possible, the CPU pauses any other processing and checks with the OS to see what new processing job is being requested.

HARD DISK

2. The operating system uses _____ to help the CPU coordinate processes that involve hardware.

3. A(n) _____ is a program that enables application programs to work with hardware devices, such as printers.

4. Operating systems allow you to work with multiple computers on a(n) _____ .

Enhancing the Operating System with Utility Software

Today s operating systems are unquestionably rich in features, but they still cannot do everything. That is why there are so many different types of utility software available. Utility software programs perform tasks that most operating systems cannot (such as detecting viruses) or extend the operating system s capabilities with additional features (such as data compression or disk defragmentation). You may not use any utility software yet, but once you see how it can improve your system s performance and protect your valuable data, you may never want to live without it again.

From the navigation menu on the left side of your browser window, choose The Operating System and Utility Software. Use this menu item s options to explore this section of the chapter. As you work through this section, answer the following questions:

1. List three of the most popular categories of utility programs:

_____

_____

_____

2. When stored on disk, a le is said to be fragmented when _____

_____ .

3. How can a defragmentation utility improve a computer s performance?

_____

_____

_____

4. List two speci c uses for data compression.

This file has been fragmented into noncontiguous sectors.

_____

_____

_____

_____

_____

_____

5. _____ is designed to help you copy large groups of files from your hard disk to some other storage media.

6. What happens to a file when you delete it?

_____

_____

_____

_____

_____

_____

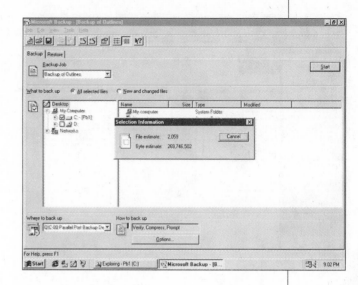

7. How does data recovery software help the user recover a file that has been deleted?

_____

_____

_____

_____

8. A virus is a parasitic program buried within another legitimate program or stored in a special area of a disk, called the _____ .

9. To locate viruses on a disk, an antivirus utility may search the _____ and _____ on the disk.

10. Screen savers were once thought to be necessary. Why? Are they still considered necessary?

_____

_____

_____

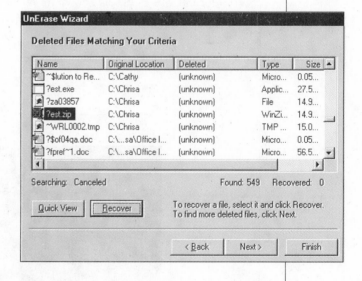

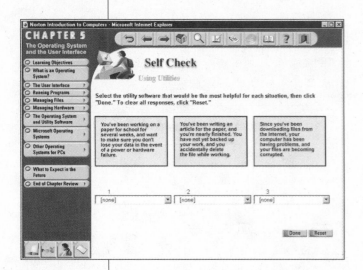

From the set of options under The Operating System and Utility Software, choose Self Check: Using Utilities. Complete the quiz on screen; follow the instructions as you go.

Microsoft Operating Systems

Although many people argue that it constitutes a monopoly, more than 80 percent of the world s PCs run on an operating system made by Microsoft. This fact illustrates not only Microsoft s ability to develop and maintain industry-standard software, but the company s marketing might, as well.

Because Microsoft operating systems are so prevalent, they merit special attention in any discussion of operating systems. This section discusses the Microsoft operating systems that are most commonly used on PCs today, and explains their differences and evolution.

From the navigation menu on the left side of your browser window, choose Microsoft Operating Systems. Use this menu item s options to explore this section of the chapter. As you work through this section, answer the following questions:

1. Despite the fact that it dominated the PC operating system market for more than a decade, MS-DOS was known more for its limitations than for its power. List three of its limitations:

_____

_____

_____

```
DEFAULT   SET       4,482  03-29-96 10:36a DEFAULT.SET
DEFAULT   SLT       7,376  03-29-96 10:30a DEFAULT.SLT
~WRM0001            35     03-01-96  1:20p ~WRM0001
CHKLIST   MS      1,674    03-29-96 10:59a CHKLIST.MS
MWAV      INI         24   03-29-96 11:00a MWAV.INI
         45 file(s)     2,002,456 bytes
          4 dir(s)    236,617,728 bytes free

C:\temp1>copy *.hlp work
DBLWIN.HLP
DOSHELP.HLP
DRVSPACE.HLP
HELP.HLP
MEMMAKER.HLP
MSBCONFG.HLP
QBASIC.HLP
SMARTMON.HLP
MSBACKUP.HLP
MSAV.HLP
MWAV.HLP
MWBACKUP.HLP
WINZIPSE.HLP
        13 file(s) copied

C:\temp1>
```

2. Early versions of Windows were not an operating system, but an operating environment. What does that mean?

_____

_____

_____

3. Although Windows 95 is a 32-bit operating system, it contains 16-bit code. What is the advantage of this?

_____

_____

_____

4. List three improvements that Windows 95 boasts over earlier versions of Windows.

_____

_____

_____

_____

_____

_____

DOS, running in a window.

A 16-bit application, designed for Windows 3.*x*.

5. _____ may be the last of Microsoft s consumer operating systems.

6. What is the advantage of the Active Desktop in Windows 98?

_____

_____

_____

7. In Windows 98, the _____ feature enables you to connect to Microsoft via the Internet and periodically update your operating system.

8. The Windows NT family is divided into two distinct products: _____ and _____ .

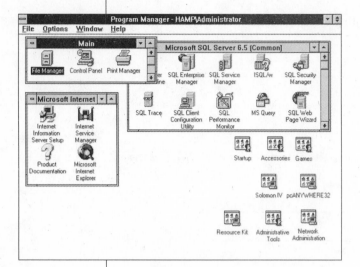

9. In what way does Windows NT Server differ from Windows NT Workstation?

_____

_____

_____

_____

_____

_____

_____

_____

10. What two characteristics of Windows CE make it ideal for use on very small hardware platforms, such as handheld computers?

_____

_____

_____

_____

Other Operating Systems for Personal Computers

Not all computers run on Microsoft operating systems. In fact, you will nd that many users of other operating systems are ercely loyal to their chosen platform,

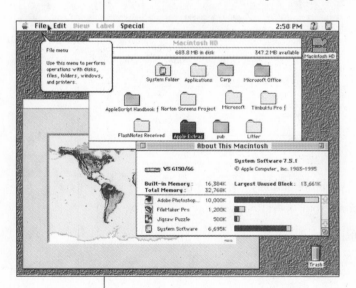

whether it is the Macintosh operating system, IBM s OS/2 Warp, or some avor of UNIX. (Ironically, Microsoft played a role in the development of both OS/2 Warp and the Macintosh OS, and markets a successful version of UNIX.) This section introduces each of these operating systems and discusses the strengths and unique features of each.

From the navigation menu on the left side of your browser window, choose Other Operating Systems for PCs. Use this menu item s options to explore this section of the chapter. As you work through this section, answer the following questions:

1. Name three reasons why the Macintosh operating system became so popular in the mid-1980s.

_____

_____

_____

2. IBM and Microsoft developed OS/2 to take advantage of the

_____ .

3. UNIX can support multiple

_____ ,

_____ , and

_____ .

From the set of options under Other Operating Systems for PCs, choose Self Check: Identifying Different Operating Systems. Complete the quiz on screen; follow the instructions as you go.

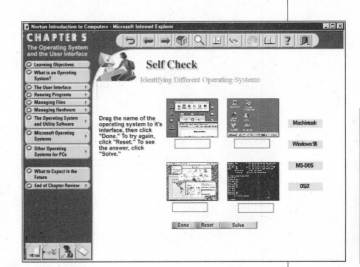

Techview

Now, review this chapter's Techview section, which discusses the use of multiple platforms. Which computing platform do you think you will use most often in your work, and why? Do you have a particular preference for one operating system over others? If so, describe your preference.

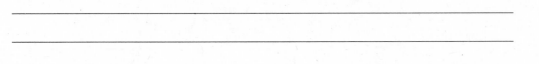

_____

_____

_____

_____

What to Expect in the Future

With each new version, operating systems get bigger as developers add new tools and functionality. Microsoft Windows is a superb example, with its networking and Internet features and a slew of capabilities that once required separate utilities. But is bigger really better? Even though the operating system is the most crucial piece of software on any computer, how much more development and improvement is needed?

From the navigation menu on the left side of your browser window, choose **What to Expect in the Future**. Study the discussion and answer the following questions:

1. Consider operating systems as they currently exist. In your view, do operating systems have enough features, tools, and capabilities, or should more be added? If you could change your operating system in any way, would you remove any of its capabilities (or make them optional)?

_____

_____

_____

2. It is clear that with Windows, Microsoft holds the lion s share of the operating systems market. Do you think this is good or bad? Why?

_____

_____

_____

Computers
In Your Career

Now, review this chapter s Computers in Your Career section, which discusses the ways in which the technologies covered in this chapter could affect your career. In the space provided here, describe the area of technology that you think might most affect your career, and explain why:

_____

_____

_____

_____

_____

_____

_____

_____

_____

_____

End of Chapter Review

The End of Chapter Review section is designed to refresh you on the major points presented in this chapter, and to test your understanding of the information.

From the navigation menu on the left side of your browser window, choose End of Chapter Review. Use the menu item s options to review the Visual Summary sections for this chapter, review the chapters Key Terms, and take the end-of-chapter quizzes.

VISUAL SUMMARIES

Review each of this chapter s Visual Summaries in turn. Each Visual Summary provides a quick overview of the major points in each section of the chapter. If you want more information about any item in a Visual Summary, click the link button next to that item, and you will return to the full discussion of that topic. (Then choose the Go Back button to return to the Visual Summary.)

KEY TERMS

Choose the Key Terms option if you need to nd the de nition for any of the important terms or concepts introduced in this chapter. To get a de nition for a term, simply look up the term in the list and click it. The term s de nition will appear in a separate window. Use this section to prepare yourself for the Key Term Quiz.

KEY TERM QUIZ

Complete the Key Term Quiz on your screen. You complete the quiz on screen, in crossword-puzzle form. When you are done with the test, choose the Solve button at the bottom of the screen. If you want to start over, choose the Reset button to clear your responses and then start again.

REVIEW QUESTIONS

Complete the Review Questions on your screen. You complete the quiz by typing correct responses in the blanks provided, selecting responses from a list, or by selecting option buttons. When you are done with the test, choose the Done button at the bottom of the screen. If you want to start over, choose the Reset button to clear your responses and then start again.

DISCUSSION QUESTIONS

Complete the Discussion Questions on your screen. You complete the quiz by typing your answers in the text boxes provided. When you are done with the test, you can print your answers and give them to your instructor. Your instructor may choose to discuss these questions in class.

*inter*NET Workshop

Do the exercises described in the Internet Workshop section. Write your ndings in the spaces provided here.

1. Did you nd any information on utilities that enable Macintosh and Windows computers to share les and disks? If so, list the products, provide a brief description of each, and list the URL where the information is located on the Web.

_____

_____

_____

_____

2. Where on the Web did you nd discussions of user interface design? What evidence did you uncover that a well-designed GUI simpli es computer use?

_____

_____

_____

_____

3. While searching the Web, did you nd information about devices that run the Windows CE operating system? What types of devices are they? What are they used for? Can you categorize the devices in any way?

_____

_____

_____

_____

4. What information can you nd on the Web about computer viruses? List the sites that provide detailed information. Then name one virus and provide a description of its behavior.

_____

_____

_____

_____

_____

CHAPTER **6**

Productivity Software

While the computer s impact has been felt in just about every aspect of our lives, its most profound affect has been in the area of personal productivity. Increasingly, people are using computers to be more productive in their profession, school work, and personal pursuits. At the heart of this phenomenon is a category of software applications called personal productivity software.

Most computer users now have several types of productivity software on their computers. Just as the name implies, productivity software can be any application that helps the user accomplish a speci c task, whether the task involves generating text or graphics, working with numbers, searching for data, or preparing a presentation. With the advent of window-based interfaces, these different applications now can work together in many ways, sharing data with one another and enabling users to perform multiple tasks simultaneously.

This chapter introduces you to the four most popular types of productivity software. They are word processing software, spreadsheet programs, database management systems, and presentation programs.

OBJECTIVES

When you complete this chapter, you will be able to do the following:

- **Name three types of documents you can create with word processing software.**
- **Name two types of editing and three types of formatting you can do in a word processor.**
- **Name and describe the four types of data that can be entered in a worksheet.**
- **Explain how cell addresses are used in spreadsheet programs.**
- **Name the two most common types of database structures and differentiate them.**
- **List six important data-management functions that can be performed in a DBMS.**
- **Describe at least six standard slide layouts provided by presentation programs.**
- **List at least four types of formatting that can be done on slides in a presentation program.**

KEY CONCEPTS

A designer may think of a CAD or graphics package as a productivity tool, or an engineer may consider a data-analysis program to be a productivity tool. But such programs are specialized and require speci c training and knowledge to be used effectively. In the mainstream of daily work, personal productivity software is used by novices and experts alike, in homes, schools, churches, and businesses. So, although just about any software package can be called productivity software, this chapter focuses on the four types of software that are used by the greatest variety of people in the widest range of situations.

Regardless of your career choice, if you work with personal computers, you probably will need (or want) to use at least one type of software described in this chapter.

Word Processing Software

- Word processing software is used to create documents that consist primarily of text, from simple letters and memos to brochures, resumes, and long documents.

- Modern word processors feature a consistent set of tools to help you navigate documents and issue commands easily. These tools include menus, toolbars, rulers, scroll bars, and others.

A business letter is an example of a simple text document, which can be quickly created and formatted in any word processor. A resume demonstrates some specialized formatting features found in word processors.

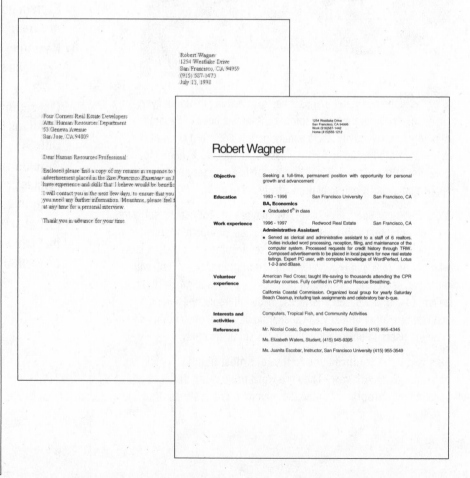

For information on **WYSIWYG**, visit this book s Web site at **www.glencoe.com/norton/online**

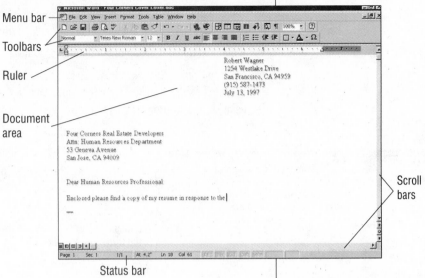

Menu bar

Toolbars

Ruler

Document area

Scroll bars

Status bar

▶ Microsoft Word's interface features tools that are common to nearly all modern word processing programs.

■ In the document area of a word processor's screen, you enter text at a blinking symbol called the insertion point. A word processor's word wrap feature automatically wraps text to the next line, so you do not need to press Enter when you reach the end of a line, unless you want to start a new paragraph.

■ Modern word processors display documents on-screen exactly as they will appear when printed. This capability has been nicknamed WYSIWYG, which stands for What You See Is What You Get.

▶ Type sizes and type styles.

This is 10 point Times New Roman type.

This is 12 point Times New Roman type.

This is 14 point Times New Roman type.

This is 16 point Times New Roman type.

This is 18 point Times New Roman type.

This is 24 point Times New Roman type.

This is 36 point Times New Roman type.

■ In word processors, a paragraph is any line or series of lines that ends with a carriage return. A paragraph can be several lines long, or only a single word.

■ The word processor has largely replaced the typewriter because it enables you to quickly correct errors and make changes without retyping an entire page. Making a change to a document is called editing.

You can make your text **bold**.

You can use *italics*, too.

Underlining is an old standby.

Sometimes you can use ~~strike through~~.

You can also use SMALL CAPS vs. LARGE CAPS.

- You can quickly erase and rekey text errors by using the Backspace and Delete keys, overtype mode, or the autocorrect feature (in many word processors).

- A block of text is a group of contiguous characters, words, lines, or paragraphs.

- To edit or format a block of text, you can select the block and then apply changes to the entire block (by making menu or toolbar choices; cutting, copying, and pasting; or by using drag-and-drop editing).

- Character formats include fonts, type size, type style, and color.

- Paragraph formats include line and paragraph spacing, indents and alignment, tabs, borders, and shading.

- Document formats include margins, page size and orientation, headers and footers, columns, and sections.

- Mail merge combines a form letter with contents from a database, creating a separate copy of the letter for each entry in the database. This technique is used to quickly produce many copies of the same letter, with each copy addressed to a different recipient.

- Modern word processors enable you to add graphics and sounds to your documents.

- Word processors also feature templates, which are predesigned documents you simply ll with text.

- Many word processing programs can create HTML documents for use on the World Wide Web.

- Desktop publishing (DTP) software features more sophisticated layout and design features than are found in word processors, and are used to design complex, multicolor, printer-ready documents.

FORM LETTER

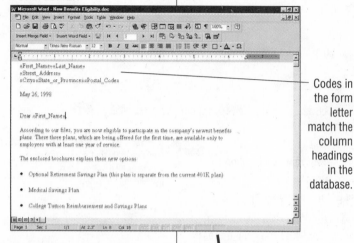

Codes in the form letter match the column headings in the database.

ADDRESS DATABASE

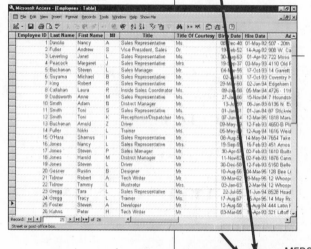

One row for each address

Performing a mail merge. ◄

MERGED LETTERS

This copy of the letter contains the name and address from one row of the address database.

NORTON Online

For information on **adding graphics to documents**, visit this book s Web site at **www.glencoe.com/norton/online**

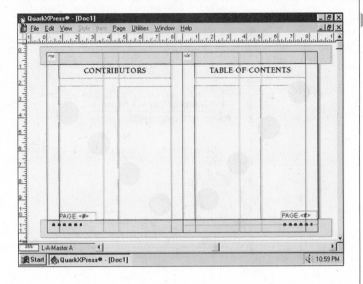

- DTP software provides advanced type controls to set type characteristics such as kerning, tracking, and leading.

- Publication designers enjoy much greater control over graphics by using DTP software, and can create master pages that act as a template for all or part of a complex document.

- DTP software enables designers to prepare documents for shipment to commercial printers, by using prepress controls. DTP software also enables designers to prepare color separations, which are required when printing multicolor documents such as magazines.

Spreadsheet Programs

- A spreadsheet program is used to calculate and analyze sets of numbers.

- A data le created with a spreadsheet is called a worksheet. You can collect multiple worksheets into a workbook.

- Like word processors, modern spreadsheet programs share many common tools and interface features, including toolbars and menus for issuing commands, scrollbars for navigating a worksheet, and more.

NORTON Online
For information on **DTP software**, visit this book s Web site at **www.glencoe.com/norton/online**

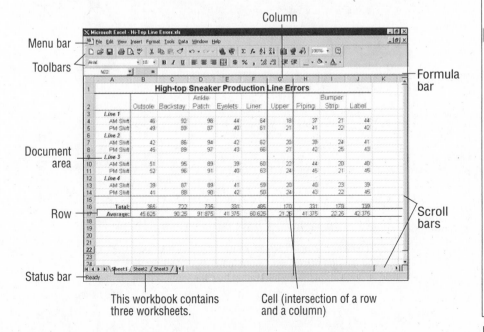

Microsoft Excel s interface features tools that are common to nearly all spreadsheets.

This workbook contains three worksheets.

Cell (intersection of a row and a column)

The active cell's
address is
displayed here.

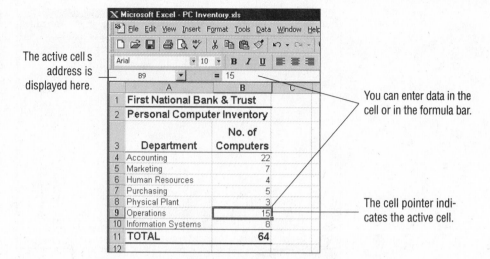

You can enter data in the
cell or in the formula bar.

The cell pointer indi-
cates the active cell.

- A worksheet is formatted in columns and rows, just like the pages of a ledger book. The intersection of each column and row forms a cell. A worksheet can contain thousands of individual cells.

- A cell's address is created by combining its column and row headings. For example, at the intersection of column B and row 4, the cell's address is B4. The active cell is high-lighted by a bold box called a cell pointer.

- Cells can contain values (any type of numerical data), labels (text), dates (calendar dates in many different formats), or formulas (mathematical operations that perform calculations based on the values and formulas in other cells).

- A formula lets you create a value in one cell that is calculated based on the values in other cells. Using 3-D worksheets, you can create calculations based on values in other worksheets.

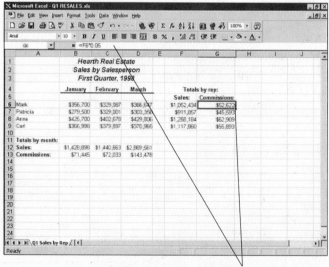

This cell contains a simple formula, which multiplies total sales
by a commission percentage. Notice that the cell displays the
results of the formula rather than the formula itself.

When this agent s sales total changes...

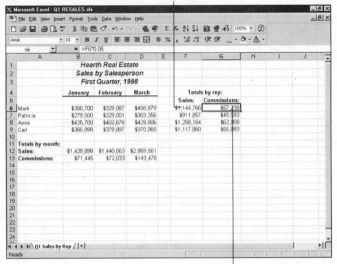

... the commission is automatically recalculated.

no comma, any number of decimal places — 23791363.25679

23,791,363.25679 — commas for thousands and millions, any number of decimal places

dollar value, with commas — $23,791,363.26

23,791,363 — bound to an integer, with commas

25.68% — percentage

23791363 — rounded to an integer, no commas

no comma, rounded to two decimal places, minus sign for negative — -23791363.26

(23,791,363.25679) — commas, negatives shown in red in parentheses (color not evident here)

▶ Eight different value formats.

- If a formula requires a value from another cell, the formula can contain a cell reference, which is the address of the referenced cell.

- Spreadsheets provide pre d e ned functions, which can perform calculations automatically without requiring the user to create a special formula. Commonly used functions are SUM, COUNT, and AVG.

- Spreadsheets can perform calculations on contiguous blocks of cells; such blocks are called ranges. Ranges can be addressed by their beginning and ending cell addresses (such as B4:D4), or can be given a name (such as May_Income).

- Numbers can be formatted as dollars, percentages, dates, times, fractions, and decimals.

- Charts are added to worksheets to make data easier to understand. The most common types of charts are bar charts, line charts, pie charts, and scatter charts.

- Spreadsheets can perform many analytical operations, such as what-if analysis and goal seeking.

▶ Chart types in Excel.

Database Management Systems

- A database is a repository for collections of related data or facts. A database management system (DBMS) is a software tool that enables users to create database tables and which provides multiple users with access to data.

- A database is based on tables of data, which like a spreadsheet are arranged in rows and columns.

A simple database of customer information, viewed as a two-dimensional table. This database is in Microsoft Access 97.

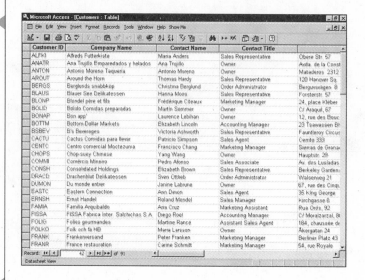

Linked elds in relational database tables.

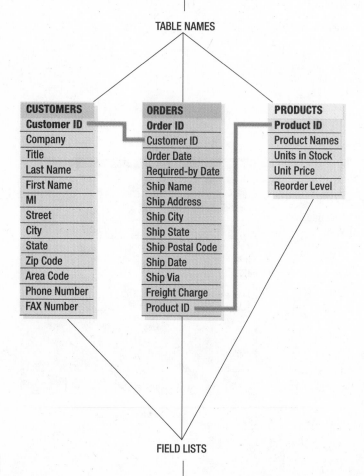

- In a database table, each row represents a record, which is a set of data for each database entry. In a database table of address information, for example, each row might be devoted to containing the address of one person. The row of data is that person s record.

- Each column represents a eld, which groups each item of data among the records into speci c categories of data. In a database table of address information, for example, each column might be devoted to containing one speci c type of information about each person, such as name, street address, city, state, ZIP code, and so on.

- Database elds can contain many different types of data, such as text, numbers, dates, time, logical descriptions (such as Yes or No), binary objects, counters, or notes.

- A at- le database is basically a two-dimensional table of elds and records. In a at- le database, one table cannot have any relationships with any other table.

- A relational database is powerful because it can consist of multiple tables, and each table can have relationships with any of the other tables; that is, elds in different tables can be linked to one another.

- Aside from at-le and relational databases, other types of databases include hierarchical databases, network databases, and object-oriented databases.

- A DBMS enables you to perform many basic data-management functions, including creating tables, entering and editing data, viewing data, sorting records, querying the database for speci c information, and generating reports from the information in the database.

- Forms are custom screens for displaying and entering data that can be associated with database tables and queries.

- Filters let you browse through selected records that meet a set of criteria.

- Sorting arranges records in a table according to speci c criteria.

▶ This form lets the user work with all the information for a single order.

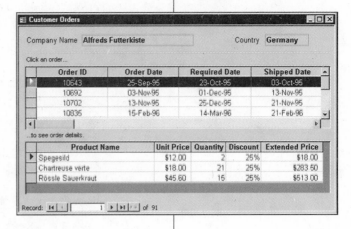

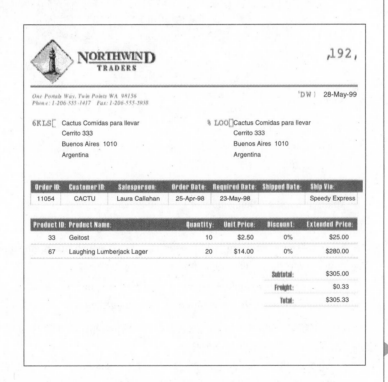

▶ This polished-looking invoice is a relatively simple database report.

- Queries are user-constructed statements that set conditions for selecting and manipulating data.

- Most DBMS programs can print specially formatted reports, based on the information provided from a query.

Presentation Programs

- Presentation programs enable you to construct individual slides, which can be organized into a series and used to support a discussion.

- Slide presentations are often displayed by using a slide projector or as overhead transparencies. Presentation programs, however, enable you to present slides directly from the PC, on the computer s monitor or on a large projection screen, using a special projector.

- Presentation programs provide a WYSIWYG interface that lets you create and edit slides on the screen just as they will appear when finished.

- Like other Windows-based applications, presentation programs enable you to work in a large document window, provide menus and toolbars for issuing commands, and feature many tools for navigating a collection of slides.

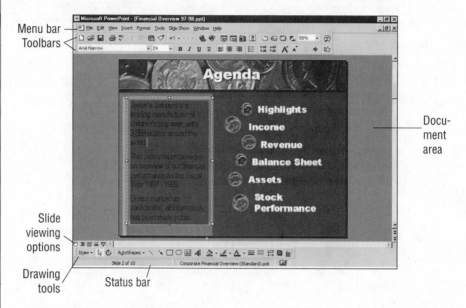

For information on **popular presentation programs**, visit this book's Web site at **www.glencoe.com/norton/online**

- A presentation can be saved as a single file containing one slide or many slides, which are used together.

- Many different types of slides are available, with different combinations of text, bullet points, graphics, boxes, and more.

- Slides can include different types of text (titles, headings, lists), charts, tables, and graphics.

For information on different **slide presentation tools**, visit this book's Web site at **www.glencoe.com/norton/online**.

- Most presentation programs provide templates, which are predesigned slides. You need only to insert the content into a template to create a presentation.

- Slides can be formatted with different fonts, colors, backgrounds, and borders. Using frames, you can resize many of the elements in a slide.

- Presentation programs enable you to add animations, sounds, and other multimedia components to your presentations.

- Using presentation software, you can present a slide show "live" from the computer's disk on a PC or video screen, instead of printing out the presentation onto 35-millimeter slides or overhead transparencies.

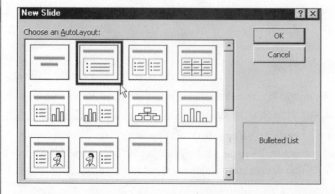

Activities

SOFTWARE THAT MAKES THE PC USEFUL

The Interactive Browser Edition introduces you to the basic types of productivity software applications that you are likely to encounter as you use a PC. As you work through Chapter 6 of the Interactive Browser Edition, you will learn about the most popular applications, their basic capabilities, and their differences.

The following sections are designed to help you navigate Chapter 6. As you work through the chapter, be sure to answer the review questions on the following pages. Write your answers directly in this book.

Word Processing Software

Aside from operating systems, word processing software is the most commonly used type of computer program. Each day, millions of people use word processors to create and edit a vast array of documents, from letters to business proposals, from recipes to resumes, from newsletters to entire books. In the past decade, word processors have evolved from basic text-only editing programs (little more than a typewriter) to sophisticated editing and design tools that provide users with multiple layout choices. If there is one type of software that you should become familiar with, it is word processing software.

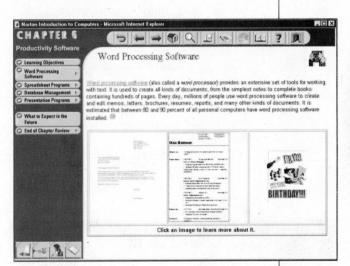

From the navigation menu on the left side of your browser window, choose Word Processing Software. Use this menu item s options to explore this section of the chapter. As you work through this section, answer the following questions:

1. List three tools that are common to most Windows-based word processing programs.

_____

_____

_____

2. What does the acronym WYSIWYG stand for, and what does it mean when we say that a word processing program is WYSIWYG?

_____

_____

3. In a word processing program, a(n) _____ shows you where the next character you type will be placed.

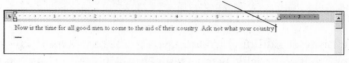

When the insertion point reaches the end of a line...

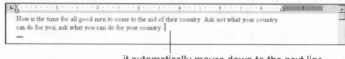

... it automatically moves down to the next line.

4. Explain the difference between overtype mode and insertion mode in a word processing program.

_____

_____

_____

_____

5. A(n) _____ is a contiguous group of characters, words, lines, sentences, or paragraphs in your document that you mark for editing.

6. List four ways you can edit a block of text in a word processing program.

_____

_____

_____

_____

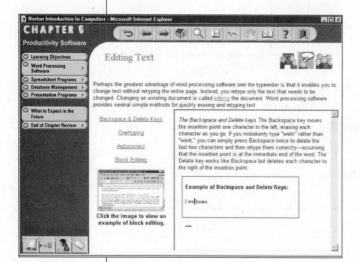

7. In word processing programs, most formatting features fall into one of three categories, which are _____, _____, and _____ .

8. The term font or typeface refers to what?

_____

_____

_____

□□□

This is the Arial font, which is proportional.

Times New Roman is a serif font.

Arial is a sans serif font.

---

9. The size of a font is measured in _____ .

10. Strikethrough, italics, and bold are examples of _____ that are commonly used in word processing programs.

11. You create a new _____ each time you press the Enter key.

12. List three types of paragraph formats that you can apply in a word processor.

_____

_____

_____

13. What is the difference between line spacing and paragraph spacing?

_____

_____

_____

14. The four paragraph alignment options are _____ ,

_____ , _____ , and

_____ .

15. A(n) _____ is a position, both on-screen and in the document, usually measured from the left margin of the document.

Left-aligned tab stop	Centered tab stop	Right-aligned tab stop	Decimal tab stop

Today's Purchases

Department	Part Code	Description	Quantity	Cost
Purchasing	44HF35	Disks	50	$12.50
Marketing	KD4323	Pens	2000	$50.25
Research	D387567	Test Tubes	1200	$2500.00
Admin	DEG776	Binder Clips	100	$50.00

16. List four types of document formats that you can create by using a word processing program.

_____

_____

_____

_____

_____

17. _____ are lines of text that run along the top of every page in a document. _____ are lines of text that run along the bottom of every page in a document.

18. What is the advantage of dividing a document into sections?

_____

_____

_____

_____

_____

19. A(n) _____ enables you to send a letter to many different people, with the correct name and address printed on each letter.

20. What are templates in a word processor, and what bene t do they provide?

_____

_____

_____

_____

_____

21. Some word processors can convert documents into _____ , so that they can be viewed in a Web browser.

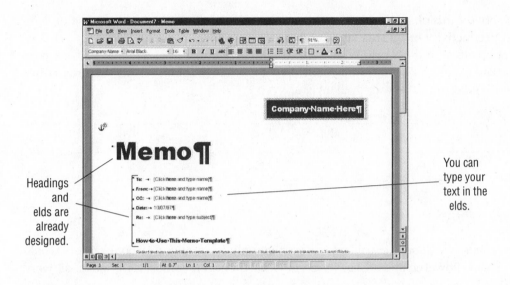

Headings and elds are already designed.

You can type your text in the elds.

22. Desktop publishing software provides four special types of controls, which generally are not found in word processing programs. What are those four controls?

_____

_____

_____

_____

_____

_____

_____

23. A(n) _____ is a special page that is set aside for de ning elements that are common to other pages in a document.

From the list of options under Word Processing Software, choose Self Check: Word Processing Software. Complete the quiz on screen; follow the instructions on the screen as you go.

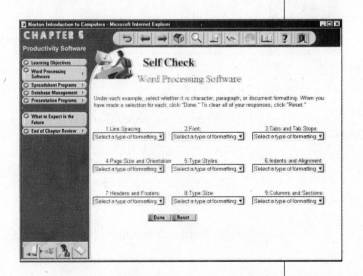

Now, review this chapter's Norton Notebook section, which discusses the use of standard productivity programs such as word processors to create HTML documents for publishing on the World Wide Web. If you were going to create and publish your own Web page, what would it be about? What types of graphics would you use to illustrate it? Who would be your audience?

_____

_____

_____

Spreadsheet Programs

Spreadsheets were once considered a tool that only accountants or bookkeepers would use. Today, however, spreadsheet programs have become almost as popular as word processors among typical computer users. People in all professions use spreadsheets to create and manage budgets, expense accounts, and inventories, and to perform other tasks that require numerical analysis, calculations, and categorizing. Spreadsheets are just as popular among home users and students as they are among professionals, and have become almost as easy to use as word processors.

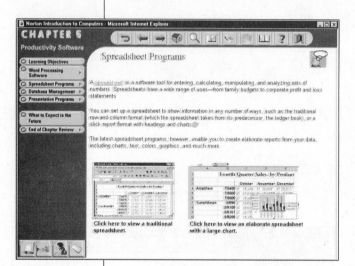

From the navigation menu on the left side of your browser window, choose Spreadsheet Programs. Use this menu item's options to explore this section of the chapter. As you work through this section, answer the following questions:

1. In a spreadsheet program, you work in a(n) _____ , and can collect one or more of them into a(n) _____ .

2. A spreadsheet's interface provides many of the same tools found in word processing programs, plus a formula bar. What can you do in the formula bar?

_____

_____

_____

3. A spreadsheet looks like a grid of _____ and _____ , which intersect to create _____ .

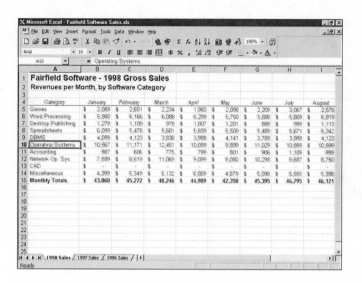

4. How does a cell get its cell address?

_____

_____

_____

_____

5. The four types of data you can enter into a worksheet's cells are

_____ , _____ ,

_____ , and _____ .

6. What is the advantage of using labels in a worksheet?

_____

_____

_____

_____

7. A(n) _____ is any number you enter into a worksheet, or which results from a computation.

8. What do formulas do in a spreadsheet?

_____

_____

_____

_____

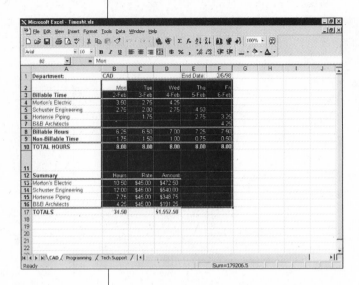

9. What is the purpose of using cell references in your spreadsheet formulas?

_____

_____

_____

10. A group of contiguous cells in a column, row, or a group of columns and rows, is called a(n) _____ .

11. In a spreadsheet, a function is a(n) _____ .

12. In the function =COUNT(C3:C7), what is the purpose of the range in parentheses?

_____

_____

_____

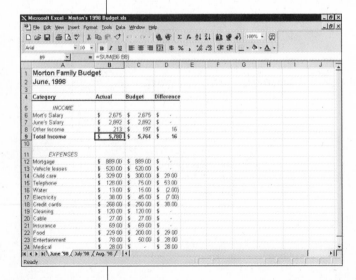

Table 6.1	Common Functions
FUNCTION NAME	**DESCRIPTION**
ABS	Absolute (positive) value of an argument
AVERAGE/AVG	Average of arguments
COUNT	Count of numbers in a range of cells
IF	Specifies a logical test to perform; then performs one action if test result is true, another if it is false
LEN/LENGTH	Number of characters in a string of characters
MAX	Maximum value of arguments
MIN	Minimum value of arguments
PMT	Periodic payment for a loan or annuity
PV	Present value of an investment
ROUND	Number rounded to a specified number of digits
SUM	Total value of arguments

13. How can you manually edit a formula in a spreadsheet program?

_____

_____

_____

14. When you move data to a new location, what happens to formulas in other cells that refer to that data?

_____

_____

_____

15. What is the difference between relative cell references and absolute cell references?

_____

_____

_____

16. The purpose of a chart is _____.

17. Why is it important to choose the right type of chart when displaying data in chart form?

_____

_____

_____

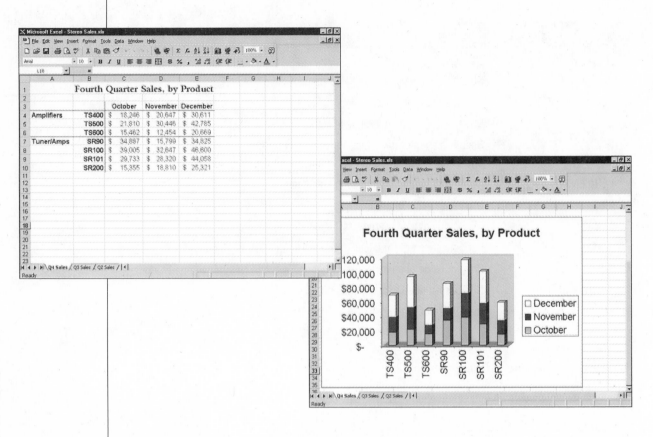

18. _____ is the process of using a spreadsheet to test how alternative scenarios affect numeric results.

19. What does goal seeking enable you to do?

_____

_____

_____

20. _____ is the process of arranging records in a specific manner.

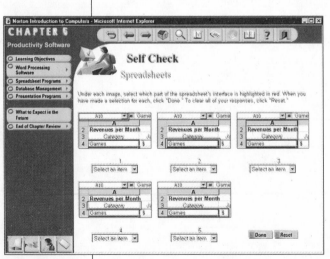

From the list of options under Spreadsheet Programs, choose Self Check: Spreadsheets. Complete the quiz on screen; follow the instructions on the screen as you go.

Productivity Tip

Now, review this chapter's Productivity Tip section, which discusses complex documents. Thinking about your own work, can you imagine a situation in which you would need to create a complex document? What type of document would it be? From what sources would the document acquire information? In your situation, which type of data sharing process (Cut/Copy/Paste, DDE, or OLE) would work best for you?

_____

_____

_____

Database Management Systems

If computers are suited to one particular task, it is managing databases. Think of any large organization—a bank, an insurance company, a phone company, a government agency—and that organization almost certainly has a large collection of data to manage. Databases can be just as important to individual computer users, such as sales professionals who must track customer and product lists.

Database management systems are important not only because they enable you to capture and record large quantities of data, but because they make the data useful. Using a well-designed database management system, you can sift through huge volumes of data to find the exact information you need. You can arrange data in many different ways, and extract all sorts of information from the data.

From the navigation menu on the left side of your browser window, choose Database Management. Use this menu item's options to explore this section of the chapter. As you work through this section, answer the following questions:

1. What is the difference between a database and a database management system (DBMS)?

_____

_____

_____

2. Telephone books, cookbooks, and address lists are examples of paper-based databases. What other types of non-computerized databases do you use regularly?

_____

_____

_____

3. In computerized databases, data is usually entered in a(n) _____ consisting of _____ and _____.

4. A database file is a(n) _____ .

5. In a database table, each row represents a record, and each column represents a field. Explain what this means, and provide a short example to illustrate your explanation.

_____

_____

_____

6. What is the key difference between a flat-file database and a relational database?

_____

_____

_____

7. The three general categories of data-management tasks are _____ , _____ , and _____ .

8. When creating a database table, you must start by defining its _____ .

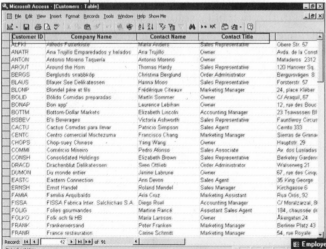

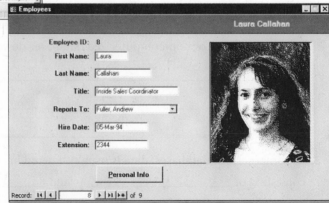

9. What type of data can each of the following field types hold?

■ Text fields: _____

■ Numeric fields: _____

■ Date or time fields: _____

■ Logical fields: _____

■ Binary fields: _____

■ Counter fields: _____

■ Memo fields: _____

10. A(n) _____ lets you display a selected list or subset of records from a database table.

11. A(n) _____ is a screen that displays data for a single record in a database.

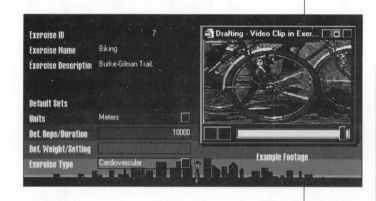

12. The two sort orders for organizing database records are

_____ and

_____ .

13. What is meant by "querying a database"?

_____

_____

_____

_____

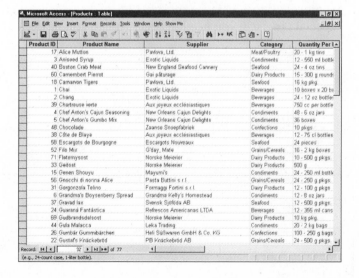

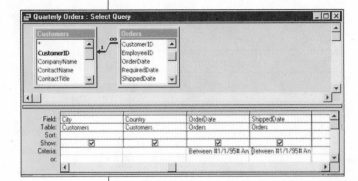

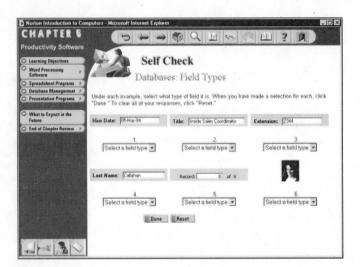

14. Two common methods of querying databases are _____ and _____ .

15. A(n) _____ is printed information that is assembled by gathering data based on user-supplied criteria. It is like a query result.

From the list of options under Database Management, choose Self Check: Databases. Complete the quiz on screen; follow the instructions on the screen as you go.

Techview

Now, review this chapter's Techview section, which discusses the ways in which software is helping small businesses succeed. Can you envision being self-employed or working in a small office or home office environment? If so, what types of software packages will you need in order to succeed? What special tasks will you need to perform that can be done with software?

_____

_____

_____

_____

_____

_____

Presentation Programs

Until a few years ago, you needed special tools and printing capabilities if you wanted to create truly professional-looking slide shows. Hours would be spent "dummying up" information, which then had to be photographed onto 35-millimeter slides or copied onto transparencies that could be shown on an overhead projector. These technologies were slow and expensive, and made it difficult to make changes to a presentation.

Modern presentation software, however, has brought the power of the slide show into the hands of millions. With a few mouse clicks, you can set up an attractive and efficient slide show that presents exactly the needed information. You can display slides in any number of ways, sometimes without printing out anything. Imaginative presenters can add animations, sounds, and other multimedia elements to slide shows that once were static and dull.

From the navigation menu on the left side of your browser window, choose Presentation Programs. Use this menu item's options to explore this section of the chapter. As you work through this section, answer the following questions:

1. _____ are single-screen images that contain a combination of text, numbers, and graphics, often on a colorful background.

2. What is a presentation template?

   _____

   _____

   _____

3. Different slide types can hold varying combinations of

   _____,

   _____,

   _____, and

   _____.

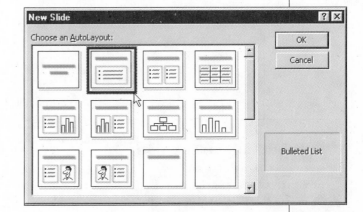

4. _____ are special resizable boxes for text and graphical elements contained in a slide.

5. How can you format text in a slide?

   _____

   _____

   _____

   _____

   _____

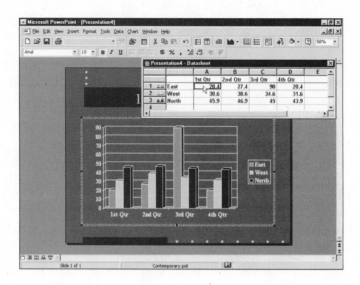

6. Why is it sometimes necessary to resize a frame or text box in a slide?

_____

_____

_____

_____

7. When creating a slide presentation, why is it important to consider the use of color?

_____

_____

_____

_____

Contributions on the rise

- 1998 contributions increased 9% over 1997
- 32% of total came from new donors
- The estate program is a success, with 312 participants in first year

8. The two ways to present slides directly from your PC's disk are to _____ _____ or _____ _____ .

9. _____ are special note text, which can be embedded in a slide.

10. Some presentation programs provide a set of _____ tools, which enable you to create slides that "build themselves" on the screen as the audience watches.

What to Expect in the Future

Although productivity software has been a boon to computer users, it has recently become the subject of much debate. Programs have more capabilities than ever and are being packaged and combined in new ways. Many users feel that programs have become too feature-rich, however, calling them "bloatware" and complaining that they require too much disk space and memory to run properly. Developers are now searching for ways to make programs smaller and faster without giving up too many features.

From the navigation menu on the left side of your browser window, choose What to Expect in the Future. Study the discussion and answer the following questions:

1. Consider the many capabilities offered by most productivity software programs. List the capabilities or features that you probably will never use, and explain why they are not necessary in your work.

   _____

   _____

   _____

   _____

   _____

   _____

   _____

   _____

   _____

2. What capabilities or features do you think are missing from productivity programs? List the features you would like to add to your favorite programs.

   _____

   _____

   _____

   _____

   _____

   _____

   _____

   _____

   _____

**Chapter 6
Hands-On Activities**

Computers
In Your Career

Now, review this chapter's Computers in Your Career section, which discusses the ways in which the technologies covered in this chapter could affect your career. In the space provided here, describe the area of technology that you think might most affect your career, and explain why:

_____

_____

_____

_____

_____

_____

_____

_____

_____

_____

_____

_____

_____

_____

_____

_____

_____

_____

_____

_____

_____

_____

End of Chapter Review

The End of Chapter Review section is designed to refresh you on the major points presented in this chapter, and to test your understanding of the information.

From the main navigation on the left side of your browser window, choose End of Chapter Review. Use the menu item's options to review the Visual Summary sections for this chapter, review the chapter's Key Terms, and take the end-of-chapter quizzes.

VISUAL SUMMARIES

Review each of this chapter's Visual Summaries in turn. Each Visual Summary provides a quick overview of the major points in each section of the chapter. If you want more information about any item in a Visual Summary, click the link button next to that item, and you will return to the full discussion of that topic. (Then choose the Go Back button to return to the Visual Summary.)

KEY TERMS

Choose the Key Terms option if you need to find the definition for any of the important terms or concepts introduced in this chapter. To get a definition for a term, simply look up the term in the list and click it. The term's definition will appear in a separate window. Use this section to prepare yourself for the Key Term Quiz.

KEY TERM QUIZ

Complete the Key Term Quiz on your screen. You complete the quiz on screen, in crossword-puzzle form. When you are done with the test, choose the Solve button at the bottom of the screen. If you want to start over, choose the Reset button to clear your responses and then start again.

REVIEW QUESTIONS

Complete the Review Questions on your screen. You complete the quiz by typing correct responses in the blanks provided, selecting responses from a list, or by selecting option buttons. When you are done with the test, choose the Done button at the bottom of the screen. If you want to start over, choose the Reset button to clear your responses and then start again.

DISCUSSION QUESTIONS

Complete the Discussion Questions on your screen. You complete the quiz by typing your answers in the text boxes provided. When you are done with the test, you can print your answers and give them to your instructor. Your instructor may choose to discuss these questions in class.

*inter*NET Workshop

Do the exercises described in the Internet Workshop section. Write your findings in the spaces provided here.

1. How did your word-processed document convert to HTML? Did it look the way you expected it to? If you wanted to create Web pages, would this type of conversion be your choice for creating them?

_____

_____

_____

2. What information did you find about macro viruses? What do they do? How can you avoid infection by a macro virus?

_____

_____

_____

3. Based on your Web research, which currently available suite of applications would you purchase? Explain the reasoning behind your selection.

_____

_____

_____

4. What kind of software did you find while searching for shareware or freeware productivity applications? Did you find any word processors, spreadsheets, or other productivity programs that impressed you? Can you compare them to commercial software? If so, how do they compare? Would you consider using a shareware or freeware package rather than a commercial package?

_____

_____

_____

5. Did you find any useful templates while searching the Internet? What programs do the templates work with? What could you use them for?

_____

_____

_____

Networks and Data Communications

OBJECTIVES

When you complete this chapter, you will be able to do the following:

- List four major benefits of connecting computers to form a network.
- Define the terms LAN, WAN, and MAN.
- List the three types of networks.
- Name the three physical topologies used to build networks.
- Name four common media for connecting the computers in a network.
- Give four reasons for connecting computers through telephone lines.
- List six common types of digital lines and the basic characteristics of each.

Whether you are sending an e-mail message to a coworker in the next office, visiting your favorite World Wide Web site, or getting some quick cash from an automated teller machine (ATM), you are using a network. A network is two or more computers—sometimes thousands—that are linked together to share data.

Networks have been a huge advancement in computer technology, and are touching our lives in many ways. For example, when you "swipe" a credit card through a card reader at a store, information about you, your purchase, and your account is exchanged between the store's computer and a computer at your bank or credit card company.

Networks come in many varieties. When most people think of a network, they imagine several computers in a single location sharing documents and devices such as printers. Networks, however, can include all the computers and devices in a department, a building, or multiple buildings spread out over a wide geographical area. When you use the Internet, you are using the world's most far-reaching computer network.

This chapter explains the basics of networking and describes the different types of networks in use today. You will learn about the specialized computers and cables that tie networks together, and see how data must be packaged in order to travel across a network. You also will learn how networks are used not only to connect computers in the same office, but also around the world.

For more
information on the
basics of networks,
visit this book's Web site at
www.glencoe.com/norton/online

KEY CONCEPTS

Few technological advances will change the way we work as much as networking will. Increasingly, isolated computer users are becoming connected to other users—whether across the Internet, a corporate network, or a direct modem connection. This not only changes the way people can communicate and work together, but it also requires users to become knowledgeable about a different computing model. To fully take advantage of a network's power and flexibility, the wise computer user becomes literate in networking terminology and philosophy, to understand what networks enable us to do and how they function.

The Uses of a Network

Most offices have a personal computer on nearly every desk. The computers are connected to form a network.

- Networks allow multiple users to have simultaneous access to shared programs and data.

- Networks also allow users to share peripheral devices, such as printers and hard disks.

- Networks usually provide users with the ability to send e-mail, and many e-mail systems let users attach files to their messages. For example, one user can send a message to another user, and attach a document file such as a memo or spreadsheet. This enables users to exchange data files without copying them to floppy disks or other external media for delivery.

  - Some networks also aid communication by providing tools for teleconferencing and videoconferencing.

  - Connecting computers to form a network makes it easier to perform backups of the data on all the networked hard disks.

By using videoconferencing software, people can participate in online conferences and see, speak, and exchange text messages with each other.

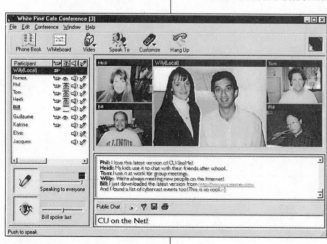

How Networks are Structured

■ A local area network (LAN) connects computers that are relatively close together, such as the computers in a single building or department.

■ A wide area network (WAN) joins LANs that are spread over a large geographical area. If a company has offices in several cities, for example, each office may have a LAN and the LANs may be connected to create a WAN. This enables workers in all offices to communicate and share data as though they were located in the same office.

■ LANs are connected to other LANs via bridges, routers, and gateways.

■ Nodes (also called clients) and a file server can be connected to create file server, client/server, and peer-to-peer networks.

NORTON Online
For more information on **LANs**, visit this book's Web site at
www.glencoe.com/norton/online

▶ A simple LAN with a file server.

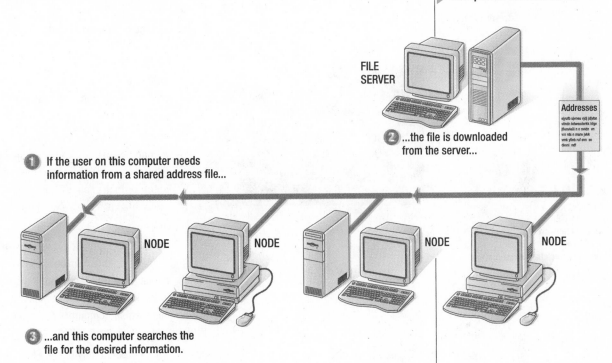

FILE SERVER

2 ...the file is downloaded from the server...

Addresses

1 If the user on this computer needs information from a shared address file...

NODE   NODE   NODE   NODE

3 ...and this computer searches the file for the desired information.

Network Topologies for LANs

■ To form a network, the individual nodes (and server, if one is used) must be connected by some means. Most network nodes are connected by some type of cable, although some network nodes are connected by wireless means. The physical layout of the cables that connect the LAN's nodes is known as the topology.

■ There are three commonly used LAN topologies: bus, star, and ring. Each topology is simply a different method of connecting the computers in a network.

■ In a bus topology, the computers are connected in serial fashion, one after another along the network cable.

■ In a star topology, the computers are connected to a central hub, not to one another.

■ In a ring topology, the nodes are connected by a single cable, which begins and ends at the same computer, forming a closed circle.

Network Media and Hardware

Twisted-pair wire. ◀

- The three most common wires used to connect computers are twisted-pair wire, coaxial cable, and fiber-optic cable.

- Increasingly, computers also communicate through wireless links; the most common types are cellular and microwave links.

- In addition to the media that connect the computers in a network, each computer also needs a network interface card.

- To communicate directly, the computers in a network must also use the same network protocol. A protocol is the language that networked computers use in order to exchange data. To communicate over the Internet, for example, computers use the TCP/IP protocol.

Fiber-optic cable. ◀

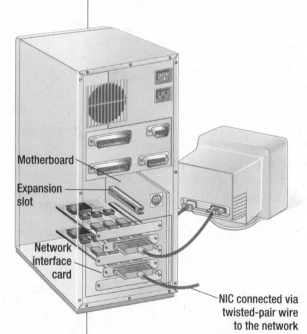

Strands of glass

- The most common network technologies are Ethernet, Token Ring, and ARCnet. These technologies enable computers to communicate over different types of networks, cabling, and so on.

- Ethernet is the most common network technology in use. A new version of Ethernet—called Fast Ethernet—enables data transmission ten times faster than is possible with standard Ethernet.

- Token Ring technology was created by IBM, and is unique because it uses a token to carry data around the network, identify computers, and determine which computers need to send and receive data.

- ARCnet technology is one of the oldest network technologies still in use. An updated version of ARCnet—called Fast ARCnet—allows for data transmission speeds that are as fast as Fast Ethernet.

NORTON Online

For more information on **wireless networking**, visit this book's Web site at **www.glencoe.com/norton/online**

Motherboard

Expansion slot

Network interface card

NIC connected via twisted-pair wire to the network

The network interface card is an expansion board that plugs into an expansion slot. It contains a jack for connecting the network cable. ◀

Network Software

- The software that manages the resources on a network is called the network operating system, or NOS.

- One popular NOS is IntranetWare, from Novell. This NOS can operate on all different types of networks and hardware platforms.

■ Other important network operating systems are Microsoft Windows NT Server, Banyan VINES, AppleShare, and Artisoft LANtastic.

An internal modem (above) and an external modem (below).

Data Communications Over Telephone Lines

■ Increasingly, phone lines are being used to send digital data because the phone system is, in effect, a pre-existing network connecting a vast number of people around the world.

■ In 1978, Hayes Microcomputer Products, Inc., introduced the first modem that allowed PC users to transmit data through a standard phone line.

■ A modem is used to translate the computer's digital signals into analog signals, which can travel over standard phone lines. A modem attached to the receiving computer translates the analog signals back into digital signals, which the computer can understand.

■ The most important consideration in choosing a modem is the speed at which it can send data, but other important considerations are the data-compression and error-correction techniques it uses, and whether the modem is internal or external.

NORTON
Online

For more
information on **ATM**,
visit this book's Web site at
www.glencoe.com/norton/online

Using Digital Telephone Lines

■ Analog phone lines are slow and not well suited for sending data, so telephone companies have gradually been switching to digital service.

■ The best known type of digital service is Integrated Services Digital Network (ISDN).

■ ISDN service is available in many urban areas, with the lowest-level service, BRI, providing a bandwidth of 128 Kbps.

■ T1 and T3 offer higher bandwidth: 1.544 Mbps and 44.736 Mbps, respectively.

■ One of the hottest buzzwords in the telecommunications industry today is Asynchronous Transfer Mode (ATM), which promises a system designed to transmit voice, data, and video data simultaneously.

Networking for the New Media

■ Multimedia networks provide high-speed access to large files, and provide large repositories for new and modified files.

■ New protocols have emerged, such as Fibre Channel Arbitrated Loop (FC-AL) and Serial Storage Architecture (SSA), that enable multiple computers to share storage media.

HOW COMPUTERS COMMUNICATE

Chapter 7 of the Interactive Browser Editon illustrates all the most commonly used networking technologies, as well as technologies used in communications via telephone lines.

The following sections are designed to help you navigate Chapter 7. As you work through the chapter, be sure to answer the review questions on the following pages. Write your answers directly in this book.

The Uses of a Network

Why are networks important? You have seen the power of the computer, now imagine the power of many computers connected and working together. Networks enable us to share information. In fact, this is why computer networks were first envisioned: to allow scientists and military officials to communicate and share information about research. In the years since the first networks, they have become commonplace—so common, in fact, that some home users have even set up two- or three-node networks in their homes.

This section explains why computer networks have become so important and common. You will learn some of the specific benefits of computer networks, and some of the unique tasks they enable users to perform.

From the navigation menu on the left side of your browser window, choose The Uses of a Network. Use this menu item's options to explore this section of the chapter. As you work through this section, answer the following questions:

1. A network is defined as:

_____

_____

_____

2. List three of the key benefits of using a network:

_____

_____

_____

3. Many users can use _____ and _____ that are stored on a shared storage device.

4. What is the incentive for a business to set up a network so that users can share peripheral devices, such as printers?

_____

_____

_____

_____

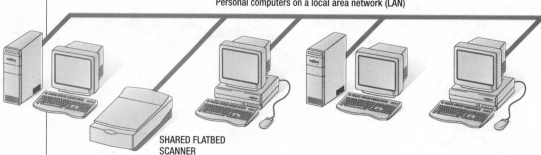

SHARED LASER PRINTER   SHARED STORAGE DEVICE

Personal computers on a local area network (LAN)

SHARED FLATBED
SCANNER

5. A document or other file that has been sent to a networked printer is known as a(n)

_____.

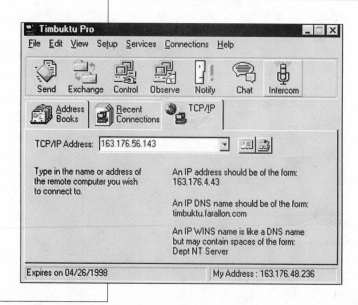

6. _____ is a system for exchanging written, voice, and video messages through a network.

7. List four advantages of using an electronic mail system.

_____

_____

_____

_____

_____

_____

8. What are the differences between teleconferencing and videoconferencing?

_____

_____

_____

9. In a network backup scenario, important files on individual users' computers are copied to a(n) _____ .

NORTON *Notebook*

Now, review this chapter's Norton Notebook section, which discusses the ways in which various organizations and businesses use networks. Select a specific business or organization in your community and describe how it might benefit from a LAN or WAN.

_____

_____

_____

How Networks are Structured

As you will see throughout this chapter, there are many types of networks and each one uses different technologies. All networks, however, share some basic concepts, rules, and terms. This section explains some of the important features that are common to all networks.

From the navigation menu on the left side of your browser window, choose How Networks are Structured. Use this menu item's options to explore this section of the chapter. As you work through this section, answer the following questions:

1. The two main types of networks, distinguished mainly by geography, are

_____ and _____ .

2. What is meant by "a LAN should be completely transparent to its users"?

3. The most distinguishing characteristic of a LAN is that its computers are

_____ .

4. In a network, data is transmitted in small groups called _____ .

5. In a packet of data, what is the importance of the header?

_____

_____

_____

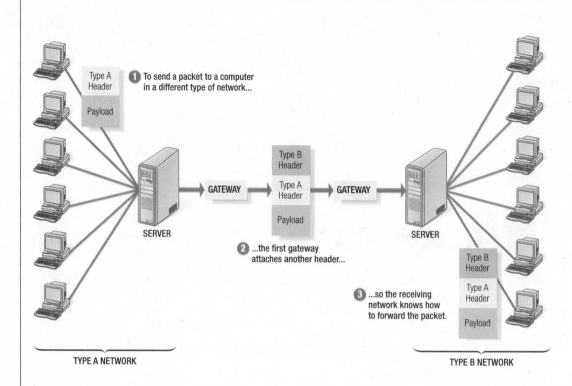

6. A(n) _____ is a set of rules and procedures that determine how a computer system receives and transmits data.

7. What is the difference between a router and a gateway?

_____

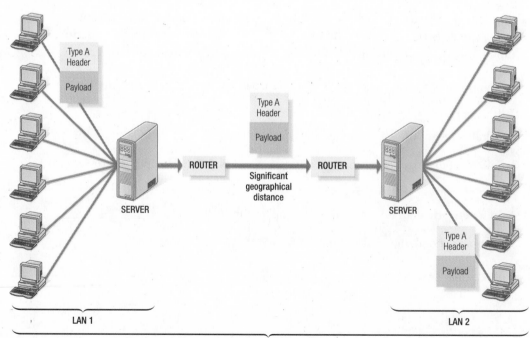

8. A(n) _____ is two or more LANs that are connected together, generally across a wide geographical area, by using high-speed or dedicated telephone lines. When confined to a single city, however, this type of network is sometimes called a(n) _____ .

9. The individual computers in a network are called _____ .

10. In a file server network, what can the nodes access?

_____

_____

_____

11. In a client/server network, the client computers provide these services:

_____

The server computer provides these services:

_____

3 The server processes the search and returns just the requested information to the client.

1 If the user on this computer needs information from a shared address file...

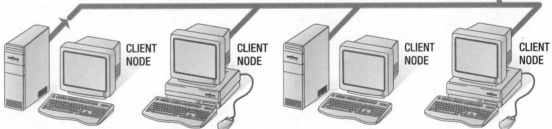

SERVER

CLIENT NODE   CLIENT NODE   CLIENT NODE   CLIENT NODE

2 ...the database search is composed on the client computer, where the user interface for the database software is running.

12. A peer-to-peer network gives users access to _____ .

Techview

Now, review this
chapter's Techview
section, which discusses remote network administration. Do some personal research
in your school or workplace and determine whether remote network administration
is being used there. If not, how could your school or business benefit by setting up
remote administration?

_____

_____

_____

Network Topologies for LANs

A local area network's computers must be connected in a specific manner, in order to
manage the flow of data, ensure that all computers participate equally in the network,
and to avoid failures in data transmission. The manner in which a network's computers
are physically connected (by cables) is called its topology; there are currently three different network topologies in use. Each of the topologies—bus, star, and ring—has its
own advantages and disadvantages, and each one is best suited for specific circumstances. This section describes each topology and explains its use.

From the navigation menu on the left side of your browser window, choose Network
Topologies for LANs. Use this menu item's options to explore this section of the chapter.
As you work through this section, answer the following questions:

1. List three factors that must be considered when choosing a network topology:

_____

_____

_____

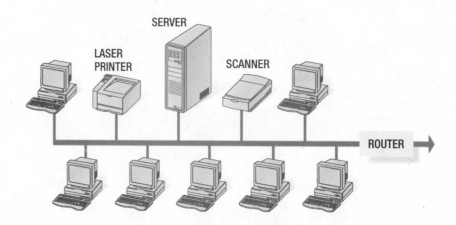

2. How are the computers in a bus network connected?

_____

_____

_____

_____

_____

3. What is the biggest disadvantage to a bus network?

_____

_____

_____

_____

_____

_____

HUB   ROUTER

LASER
PRINTER

4. What is the main distinguishing factor found in a star network?

_____

_____

_____

_____

5. List two advantages provided by the hub in a star network.

_____

_____

_____

_____

6. How are computers connected in a ring network?

_____

_____

_____

_____

Chapter 7
Hands-On Activities

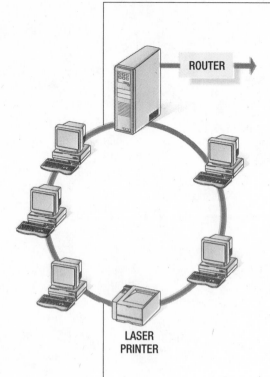

ROUTER →

LASER
PRINTER

7. In a ring network, how is data transmitted from the sending computer to the receiving computer?

_____

_____

_____

_____

_____

_____

_____

8. Why is there no danger of data collisions in a ring network?

_____

_____

_____

_____

_____

_____

_____

Network Media and Hardware

To set up a network, you need more than just a group of computers. To communicate with one another, networked computers need a means of sharing data—a medium, such as cables or wireless transmitters and receivers. Inside the computer, a special card is needed to attach the computer to the network. Depending on the circumstances, other specialized types of hardware may be required, as well. This section introduces you to the most commonly used types of network cable, wireless links, network interface cards, and more.

From the navigation menu on the left side of your browser window, choose Network Media and Hardware. Use this menu item's options to explore this section of the chapter. As you work through this section, answer the following questions:

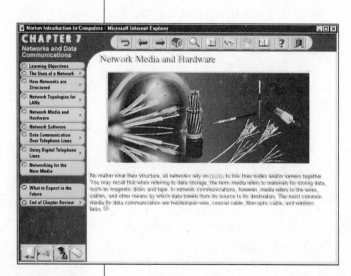

1. What is meant by the term "media" when used in networking?

_____

_____

_____

_____

_____

2. The four most common media in data communications are _____,

_____ , _____ , and

_____ .

3. What is the difference between shielded and unshielded twisted-pair wire? What purpose does shielding serve?

_____

_____

_____

_____

_____

4. Define the term "bandwidth." Why do you think bandwidth is so important as a measurement of network performance?

_____

_____

_____

_____

_____

_____

_____

_____

_____

_____

5. List two advantages of coaxial cable, compared to twisted-pair wire.

_____

_____

_____

6. Fiber-optic cable transmits data in the form of _____ , and can transmit data at a rate of _____ .

7. Wireless communication relies on _____ or _____ for transmitting data.

8. A network interface card is _____ .

9. What is a network protocol, and why are protocols required?

_____

_____

_____

10. The four most common types of network technology are _____ , _____ , _____ , and _____ .

11. The most commonly used network technology is _____ .

12. How does Token Ring networking work?

_____

_____

_____

_____

_____

_____

_____

_____

_____

From the set of options under Network Media and Hardware, choose Self Check: Building a Network. Complete the quiz on screen; follow the instructions on the screen as you go.

Norton Introduction to Computers - Microsoft Internet Explorer

CHAPTER 7
Networks and Data Communications

- Learning Objectives
- The Uses of a Network
- How Networks are Structured
- Network Topologies for LANs
- Network Media and Hardware
- Network Software
- Data Communication Over Telephone Lines
- Using Digital Telephone Lines
- Networking for the New Media
- What to Expect in the Future
- End of Chapter Review

Self Check

Building a Network

Your small company has decided to network it's computers, and it's up to you to design the network. There are about 30 employees, all working out of one several-story office building. Your company needs a network mostly to collaborate on small projects, produce reports, send e-mail, and share a laser printer; there's no real need to transmit large amounts of data. There is one problem: your boss is concerned about the financial impact of lots of new equipment and lost time while the network is being set up. You need something simple and reliable.

Select the best choice from each category (going across), then click Done.

LAN	WAN	MAN
File Server	Client/Server	Peer-to-Peer
Bus	Star	Ring
Twisted Pair	Coaxial	Fiber Optic	Wireless
Ethernet	Fast Ethernet	Token Ring	ARCnet

Done   Next Question

Network Software

In previous chapters, you learned that a computer is basically useless without software to run it. The same is true of a network. Special network operating system (NOS) software is required to manage the network-specific hardware and the operation of the network. An individual computer's operating system manages the computer's hardware, processing, and files; an NOS does this on a larger scale.

From the navigation menu on the left side of your browser window, choose Network Software. As you work through this section, answer the following questions:

1. What is the purpose of network operating system software?

_____

_____

_____

_____

_____

_____

_____

_____

_____

_____

_____

_____

2. Three of the most popular network operating systems currently in use are

_____ ,

_____ , and

_____ .

Data Communication over Telephone Lines

Networks have resulted in an entirely new way of working. Sharing information and hardware resources is now simple, if computer users are linked together by a network. What happens, however, if two users are not connected to the same network? Can they still share data, especially if they are separated by a great distance?

The answer is yes, thanks to the telephone lines that lace the planet. Because this worldwide system of lines is already a network in itself, it can be used to connect computers, as well as telephones. If your computer has a modem and you can access a telephone line, you can interact with other similarly equipped users in the world's largest network.

From the navigation menu on the left side of your browser window, choose Data Communication over Telephone Lines. Use this menu item's options to explore this section of the chapter. As you work through this section, answer the following questions:

1. How are telephone lines different from the dedicated media used in networks?

_____

_____

_____

2. A(n) _____ is required to attach a computer to an analog telephone line.

3. What is the basic function of a modem?

_____

_____

_____

_____

4. The correct unit of measurement when determining a modem's transmission speed is _____ , not _____ .

5. What role does data compression play in data communications via modems?

_____

_____

_____

_____

6. Modems come in three forms. What are they? _____,

_____ , and _____ .

7. Name three common uses for data communication over phone lines.

_____

_____

_____

FULL-DUPLEX TRANSMISSION

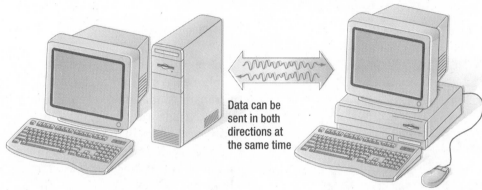

Data can be
sent in both
directions at
the same time

HALF-DUPLEX TRANSMISSION

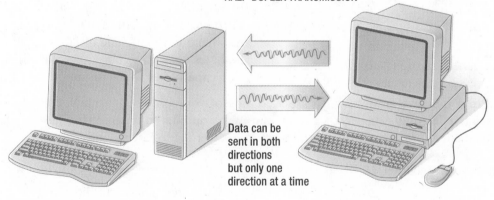

Data can be
sent in both
directions
but only one
direction at a time

8. Direct connections between two users over phone lines are becoming less frequent. Why?

_____

_____

_____

9. What is a File Transfer Protocol, and why are such protocols necessary?

_____

_____

_____

Chapter 7
Hands-On Activities

10. What is the difference between uploading and downloading?

_____

_____

_____

_____

From the set of options under Data Communication over Telephone Lines, choose Self Check: Modems. Complete the quiz on screen; follow the instructions on the screen as you go.

Using Digital Telephone Lines

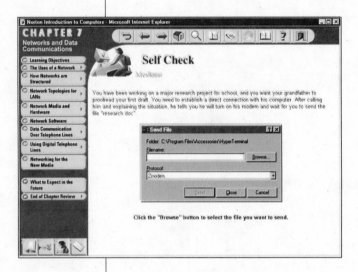

In the previous section, you learned that analog telephone lines are not well suited to the task of transmitting digital signals, even though they are frequently being used for that task. Despite advances in modem technology, analog lines cannot deliver data as rapidly as digital lines can. For this reason, many telephone companies have made dedicated data lines available to their customers. There are several types of digital lines, varying widely in transmission speeds and cost. This section introduces you to the types of digital lines now in common use and discusses new technologies that may increase data transmission capabilities in the future.

From the navigation menu on the left side of your browser window, choose Using Digital Telephone Lines. Use this menu item's options to explore this section of the chapter. As you work through this section, answer the following questions:

1. Using modems, analog lines can transmit data at speeds of up to

_____ . Typical network transmission speeds, however, are at a

speed of at least _____ .

2. After all analog telephone lines have been converted to digital lines, will you still need a modem to transmit data?

_____

_____

_____

_____

3. ISDN lines feature two lines that can carry voice and data, and which can be used together, enabling the user to _____ .

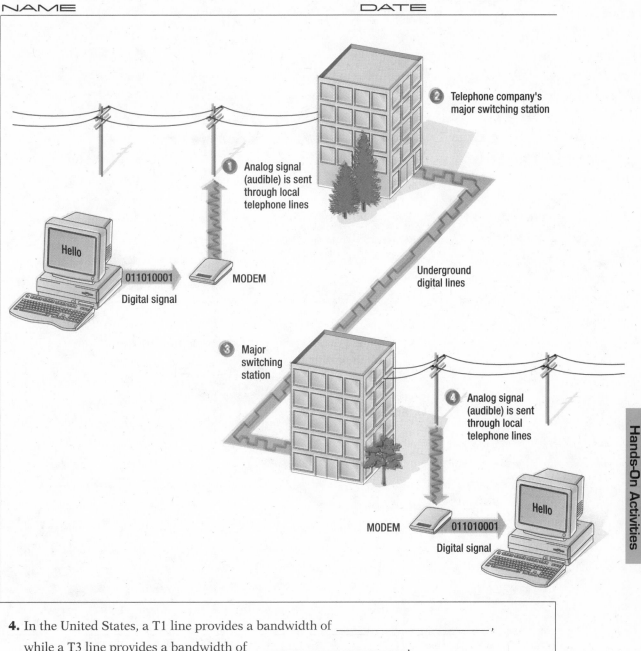

Telephone company's major switching station ②

① Analog signal (audible) is sent through local telephone lines

Hello

011010001 → MODEM

Digital signal

Underground digital lines

③ Major switching station

④ Analog signal (audible) is sent through local telephone lines

MODEM 011010001

Digital signal

Hello

4. In the United States, a T1 line provides a bandwidth of _____ , while a T3 line provides a bandwidth of _____ .

5. Although ISDN, T1, and T3 lines are fast, _____ is being developed as a more efficient digital line for transmitting video and audio signals as well as data.

6. How does ATM technology promise to solve the bandwidth problem inherent in transmitting digital data across phone lines?

_____

_____

_____

_____

_____

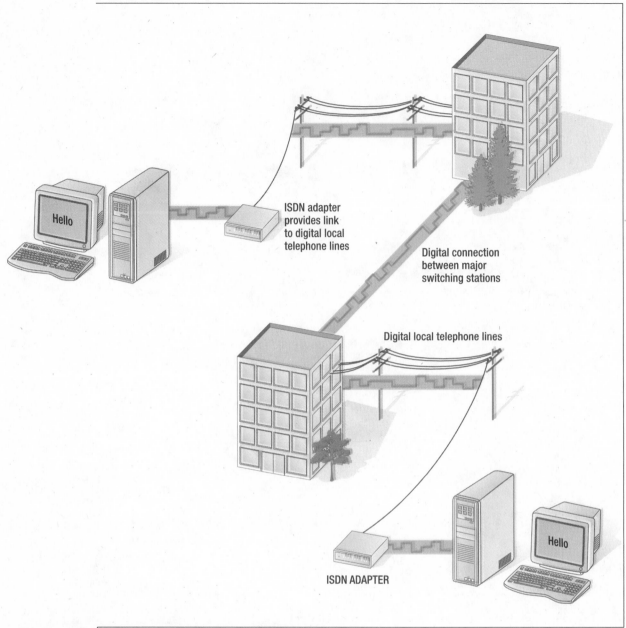

ISDN adapter
provides link
to digital local
telephone lines

Digital connection
between major
switching stations

Digital local telephone lines

ISDN ADAPTER

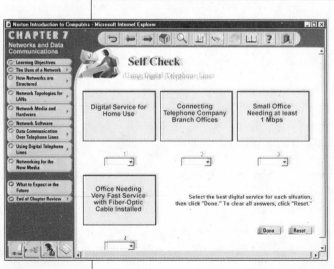

From the set of options under Using Digital
Telephone Lines, choose Self Check: Using
Digital Telephone Lines. Complete the quiz on
screen; follow the instructions on the screen
as you go.

Productivity Tip

Now, review this chapter's Productivity Tip section, which discusses network computers. Considering the way you plan to use computers in your own career, do you think that you will ever use a network computer in your job? Do you think you would benefit from using a network computer rather than a personal computer? Explain why or why not.

_____

_____

_____

Networking for the New Media

As more and more companies incorporate new media (also called multimedia) technologies into their businesses, networks are being pushed beyond their capacities, in terms of both storage and bandwidth. New networking technologies are now emerging that will enable multimedia developers and users to store and share new media tools and content—including audio, video, animation, and other types of files—without bogging down the network.

From the navigation menu on the left side of your browser window, choose Networking for the New Media. As you work through this section, answer the following questions:

1. A(n) _____ must provide high-speed access to large files, in addition to providing large repositories for new and modified files.

2. What do protocols such as Fibre Channel Arbitrated Loop (FC-AL) and Serial Storage Architecture (SSA) do?

_____

_____

_____

_____

What to Expect in the Future

The 1990s have seen an explosion in connectivity. Millions of businesses—large and small alike—have networked their internal computer systems, with more networks being configured every day. Nearly 20 million people use online services to access the Internet, with nearly 100 million connected via an ISP. Entire networks are being interconnected, and organizations of all kinds are taking advantage of this phenomenon to create intranets, extranets, and Web sites. This growth is not expected to slow down until well after the turn of the century, and the demand for improvements in network technology, performance, and ease of use certainly will not abate any time soon.

Chapter 7
Hands-On Activities

From the navigation menu on the left side of your browser window, choose What to Expect in the Future. Study the discussion, and then answer the following questions:

1. In the workplace or in the school, what do you think are the main advantages to using a network?

_____

_____

_____

2. Infloglut is one of the primary drawbacks to global networking. What other drawbacks can you think of?

_____

_____

_____

3. How do you think networking will affect you in the workplace? Will it be an advantage to you in your chosen field, or have no impact? Why?

_____

_____

_____

Computers
In Your Career

Now, review this chapter's Computers in Your Career section, which discusses the ways in which the technologies covered in this chapter could affect your career. In the space provided here, describe the area of technology that you think might most affect your career, and explain why:

_____

_____

_____

_____

_____

_____

_____

_____

End of Chapter Review

The End of Chapter Review section is designed to refresh you on the major points presented in this chapter, and to test your understanding of the information.

From the navigation menu on the left side of your browser window, choose End of Chapter Review. Use the menu item's options to review the Visual Summary sections for this chapter, review the chapter's Key Terms, and take the end-of-chapter quizzes.

VISUAL SUMMARIES

Review each of this chapter's Visual Summaries in turn. Each Visual Summary provides a quick overview of the major points in each section of the chapter. If you want more information about any item in a Visual Summary, click the link button next to that item, and you will return to the full discussion of that topic. (Then choose the Go Back button to return to the Visual Summary.)

KEY TERMS

Choose the Key Terms option if you need to find the definition for any of the important terms or concepts introduced in this chapter. To get a definition for a term, simply look up the term in the list and click it. The term's definition will appear in a separate window. Use this section to prepare yourself for the Key Term Quiz.

KEY TERM QUIZ

Complete the Key Term Quiz on your screen. You complete the quiz on screen, in crossword-puzzle form. When you are done with the test, choose the Solve button at the bottom of the screen. If you want to start over, choose the Reset button to clear your responses and then start again.

REVIEW QUESTIONS

Complete the Review Questions on your screen. You complete the quiz by typing correct responses in the blanks provided, selecting responses from a list, or by selecting option buttons. When you are done with the test, choose the Done button at the bottom of the screen. If you want to start over, choose the Reset button to clear your responses and then start again.

DISCUSSION QUESTIONS

Complete the Discussion Questions on your screen. You complete the quiz by typing your answers in the text boxes provided. When you are done with the test, you can print your answers and give them to your instructor. Your instructor may choose to discuss these questions in class.

*inter*NET Workshop

Do the exercises described in the Internet Workshop section. Write your findings in the spaces provided here.

1. List the names and URLs of the Web sites you found that discuss peer-to-peer networking, and the advantages and disadvantages of using peer-to-peer networking in a small business or office environment. What conclusion did you reach after reviewing the information provided by these Web sites?

_____

_____

_____

_____

2. List the names and URLs of the Web sites you found that discuss network cabling. By reviewing the information provided at these sites, what did you learn about the network cabling system used in your school or company?

_____

_____

_____

_____

3. Based on your findings on the Internet, what are the advantages of taking and passing the Microsoft or Novell certification program?

_____

_____

_____

4. Using information you have gathered from the Web, list and compare the specifications for two different modems:

Feature	Modem 1	Modem 2
Brand	_____	_____
Model	_____	_____
Price	_____	_____
Internal/External?	_____	_____
Speed	_____	_____
Protocols used	_____	_____
Compression techniques	_____	_____

CHAPTER **8**

The Internet and Online Resources

OBJECTIVES

When you complete this chapter, you will be able to do the following:

- Give two reasons why the Internet got started.
- Describe the two parts of an Internet address.
- Name the nine features of the Internet.
- List two ways in which a PC can access the Internet.

The Internet has exploded into the world's consciousness in a manner unparalleled in the history of computing. With the development of the World Wide Web in the early 1990s, this relatively unknown national resource skyrocketed into prominence as computer users scrambled to set up e-mail accounts, install browsers, and "surf the Net." Hardware and software manufacturers saw the Internet as a growth market, and quickly began developing new products (and adapting existing ones) that were "Internet-ready," "Internet-compatible," or at least "Internet-aware."

As a collection of interconnected networks, the Internet is both vast in scope and limitless in potential as a means of global communication. Each week, it seems, a new technology emerges that creates new opportunities for Internet use, makes the Web more useful, and enhances our online experience in some manner.

Despite its vastness and technological complexity, however, the Internet and its primary features are relatively easy to master and use. Connecting to the Internet is now a pretty simple process, and Internet software (browsers, e-mail packages, FTP clients, etc.) are continually being improved and made easier to use.

This chapter introduces you to the Internet, its history, and its major features. You will understand not only how the Internet works and how to access it, but which tools are essential for productive "surfing."

NORTON Online

For information on the **history of the Internet**, visit this book's Web site at www.glencoe.com/norton/online

KEY CONCEPTS

Many computer users attempt to jump into the Internet without first learning what it is all about. This can be a mistake; if you do not know how the Internet works, how data travels across it, and how its features work, you can easily become frustrated. Because the Internet can be such an intimidating place, and because it is easy to get lost while surfing, a little information can be very helpful.

Background and History: An Explosion of Connectivity

- The Internet was created for the U.S. Department of Defense as a tool for military communications, command and control, and exchanges of data with defense contractors. To create this giant, nationwide network, the DOD connected computers at various universities and defense contractors.

- In its earliest form, the Internet was used primarily by scientists and the military as a means for communicating and exchanging information.

- The Internet has continued to expand and grow by establishing interconnections with other networks around the world.

- Today, the Internet is a network of networks that is interconnected through regional and national backbone connections.

- The Internet carries messages, documents, programs, and data files that contain every imaginable kind of information for businesses, educational institutions, government agencies, and individual users.

- The Internet connects millions of computers around the world. There is no central ownership or management of the Internet; it is a cooperative community in which all resources are shared.

How the Internet Works

- To communicate with one another, all computers on the Internet must use the same protocols, which are rules and procedures that control timing and data format. On the Internet, all computers use the Transmission Control Protocol/Internet Protocol (TCP/IP).

- Any computer on the Internet can communicate with any other computer on the Internet. Typically, the two computers do not connect directly to one another. Rather, they connect to local and regional networks, which are connected together through the Internet backbone.

- A computer can connect directly to the Internet, or as a remote terminal on another computer, or through a gateway from a network that does not use TCP/IP.

- Every computer on the Internet has a unique Internet Protocol (IP) address, which is a unique address composed of a series of numbers. Although an IP address—such as 205.46.117.104—is unique and can easily be stored in an address database, it can be very difficult for people to remember.

- Most computers also have an address that uses the Domain Name System (DNS) method of addressing, which uses words rather than numbers. Domain names are categorized by the type of organization at the address. For example, the University of Washington's DNS address is *washington.edu* (*edu* stands for "education") and Microsoft's is *microsoft.com* (*com* stands for "commercial").

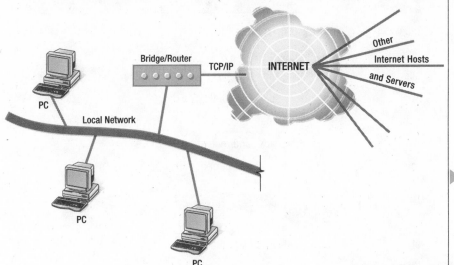

For information
on **listservs**, visit
this book's Web site at
www.glencoe.com/norton/online

▶ A typical Internet connection.

- Domain name addresses can be divided into subdomains, so that different computers within a domain can have separate, unique names. At the genetics department at the University of Washington, for example, the DNS address might be *genetics.washington.edu.*

- Domain names also sometimes include an identifier that indicates the country where the computer is located. If a company is located in France, for example, its domain name might be *companyname.com.fr.*

- DNS and IP addresses identify computers, but any computer can have several users. Each user can have an account on the computer, and this account name usually serves as the user's e-mail address, as in *jsmith@microsoft.com.*

- Most Internet application programs use the client-server model; users run client programs that obtain data and services from a server.

Major Features of the Internet

- The Internet is a source of news, business communication, entertainment, and technical information. It also supports "virtual communities," which are made up of people who share an interest, such as a hobby or political viewpoint.

- Electronic mail (e-mail) is the most popular use of the Internet. With e-mail software, a user can send a message to another individual user or to many users.

- Mailing lists—called listservs—enable users to post messages, which are automatically sent to all users on the list.

- News groups and mailing lists are conferences distributed through the Internet and other electronic networks. Like listserv groups, users of a news group

Table 8.1	Internet Domains
DOMAIN	**TYPE OF ORGANIZATION**
com	business (commercial)
edu	educational
gov	government
mil	military
net	gateway or host
org	other organization

▶ An e-mail message.

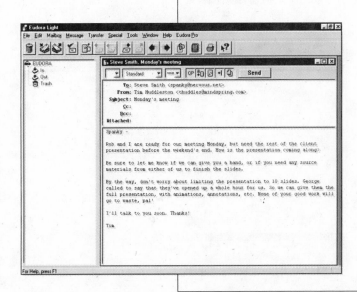

Table 8.2	Common Usenet Domains
DOMAIN	**DESCRIPTION**
comp	Computer-related topics
sci	Science and technology (except computers)
soc	Social issues and politics
news	Topics related to Usenet
rec	Hobbies, arts, and recreational activities
misc	Topics that do not fit one of the other domains
The Most Important Alternative Topics Include	
alt	Alternative news groups
bionet	Biological sciences
biz	Business topics, including advertisements
clari	News from the Associated Press and Reuters, supplied through a service called Clarinet
k12	News groups for primary and secondary schools

share an interest. Instead of e-mailing messages to the group, however, news group users post messages publicly, for all other users to read and respond to. The messages are stored on servers throughout the Internet.

■ Telnet allows a user to operate a second computer from the keyboard of his or her machine. Telnet is helpful in many ways; for example, you can use Telnet to log into the computer systems of many large libraries, to obtain information about books.

■ File Transfer Protocol (FTP) is the Internet tool for copying data and program files from one computer to another.

■ Many FTP sites require users to have a password in order to access their systems, but many other sites allow users to enter and retrieve files anonymously.

■ Although FTP is simple to use, it is not possible for one person to keep track of all the files that are available on all FTP servers. Therefore, users can use a system called Archie (which stands for archives), a searchable index of FTP archives, to locate files.

■ Gopher is a hierarchical menu system that helps users find resources that may be anywhere on the Internet.

■ Internet Relay Chat (IRC) enables users to communicate with one another in real-time while online. Chats are public conferences, conducted in real-time, for which people join channels to discuss topics of interests. In a chat session, when a user types at his or her computer, the characters appear on the screens of other users.

A Telnet connection to a library catalog.

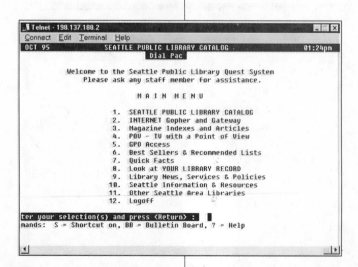

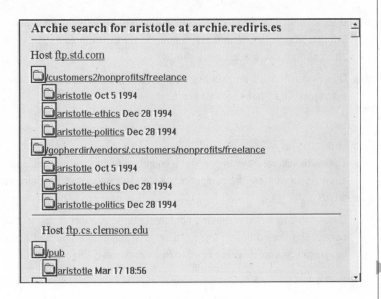

Archie search for aristotle at archie.rediris.es

Host ftp.std.com

📁 /customers2/nonprofits/freelance
  📁 aristotle Oct 5 1994
  📁 aristotle-ethics Dec 28 1994
  📁 aristotle-politics Dec 28 1994
📁 /gopherdir/vendors/.customers/nonprofits/freelance
  📁 aristotle Oct 5 1994
  📁 aristotle-ethics Dec 28 1994
  📁 aristotle-politics Dec 28 1994

Host ftp.cs.clemson.edu

📁 /pub
  📁 aristotle Mar 17 18:56

▶ Results of an Archie search for files related to "Aristotle."

■ The World Wide Web (WWW) combines text, graphics, and links to millions of documents. The Web is the fastest-growing part of the Internet.

■ In Web documents, users can click hypertext links to "jump" to other resources on the Web. A link may lead to another part of the same document, a different document, or a completely different Web site.

■ The Web operates on a special protocol—the Hypertext Transfer Protocol (HTTP)—which is designed to support hyperlinks. Individual Web pages are written in a page-description language called Hypertext Markup Language (HTML), which contains the codes that enable a Web browser to read the page and jump to other linked documents.

■ Web pages use special addresses, called uniform resource locators (URLs). The URL tells your computer where the page is located.

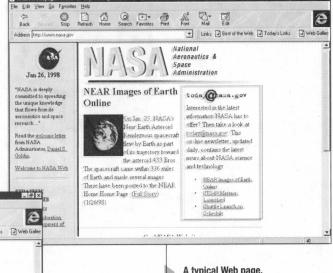

▶ A typical Web page.

▶ America Online (AOL) is an online service that offers a variety of information and services, including access to the Internet.

For information
on **PPP**, visit this
book's Web site at
www.glencoe.com/norton/online

- Online service companies and bulletin board services (BBSs) offer, in addition to Internet access, a wide variety of other features, such as e-mail, discussion groups, stock quotes, news, and online games.

- Other Internet tools and services can be integrated into word processors, database managers, and other application programs.

Accessing the Internet

- There are several ways to connect a computer to the Internet. The appropriate method depends on whether the computer is a stand-alone system or is already connected to a LAN.

- Users can connect stand-alone computers through a direct connection. This involves connecting the computer's serial port to a telephone line and using a Serial Line Interface Protocol (SLIP) or Point to Point Protocol (PPP) connection.

A remote terminal connection to a shell account.

```
ls-1Rt
ls-1Rt.Z
00WELCOME.info
Copyright.info
226 Transfer complete.
243 bytes received in 0.02 seconds (9.96 Kbytes/s)
ftp> get README.online
200 PORT command successful.
150 Opening ASCII mode data connection for README.online (1880 bytes).
226 Transfer complete.
local: README.online remote: README.online
1929 bytes received in 0.36 seconds (5.22 Kbytes/s)
ftp> bye
221 Goodbye.
linex2> ls
Mail/          News/          brian/          public_html/
Mailboxes/     README.online  mail/           sandstone/
linex2> sz README.online
sz: 1 file requested:
README.online

Sending in Batch Mode
**B00000000000000
linex2>
```

- Using a shell account, a user can connect to a host computer on the Internet and exchange commands and data in ASCII text format.

- The most common connection method for stand-alone computers is a gateway connection, in which the computer connects via a telephone line to an Internet Service Provider (ISP) host computer.

- LANs that already use TCP/IP protocols can easily connect to the Internet, via a router.

Connecting a PC to the Internet

- The Winsock standard specifies the Windows interface between TCP/IP applications and network connections.

- Users can mix and match Winsock-compatible applications.

- Internet application suites are available from many suppliers; these suites combine a full set of applications and drivers in a single package.

Working on the Internet

■ Businesses that connect their networks to the Internet often set up firewalls to prevent unauthorized users from gaining access to proprietary information.

■ As more companies sell products and services over the Web, security is an increasingly important issue. Developers are creating stronger measures to protect personal data, such as e-mail addresses and credit card numbers, which consumers often must provide over the Web.

■ Improved encryption techniques are helping to protect sensitive information on the Internet.

■ Many legal issues continue to arise concerning the use of the Internet by individuals. These include the protection of copyrights, the privacy of e-mail, and the availability of pornographic material to minors.

Overview of Browsers

■ Web browsers are applications used to navigate and view documents on the Web.

■ Netscape Navigator and Microsoft Internet Explorer are the two most popular Web browsers, with a combined market share of over 90 percent.

■ Navigator is available in several versions; the latest is version 4, which is available either as a stand-alone product or as part of the Netscape Communicator suite of Internet tools.

■ Communicator includes not only Navigator, but also an e-mail client, a Web page editor, a news reader, a push client, and other tools.

■ Explorer supports e-mail, news groups, Web page creation, and push technology.

■ Internet Explorer is also currently available in version 4 and is free.

NORTON Online
For information on **Internet products**, visit this book's Web site at **www.glencoe.com/norton/online**

Table 8.3	Web Browser Comparison Chart	
FEATURE	**INTERNET EXPLORER 4**	**COMMUNICATOR 4**
HTML 3.2	Yes	Yes
HTML editing	With FrontPage Express	With Composer
Cascading style sheets	Yes	Yes
E-mail	Yes	Yes
News reader	Yes	Yes
Online conferencing	No	Yes
Web view	Yes	No
VBScript	Yes	No
JavaScript	Yes	Yes
Plug-ins	As ActiveX Controls	Yes
Offline browsing	Yes	No
Java	Yes	Yes
ActiveX	Yes	Yes
Dynamic Web pages	Yes	Yes

Netscape Communicator 4 is an
all-in-one Internet tool that you
can use for Web browsing,
e-mail, joining news groups,
and much more.

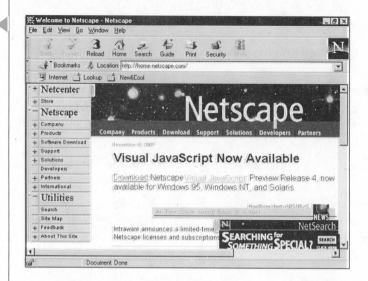

■ Both Navigator and Explorer support Java, ActiveX technology, plug-ins, and a host of other features.

Commerce on the Web

■ Commerce on the Web has grown from a Web site selling flowers to an estimated 250,000-plus business sites devoted to selling products and services.

■ Electronic commerce (e-commerce) on the Web is expected to hit $120 billion by the year 2000.

■ Electronic commerce advocates envision a world where business will be conducted online directly from business to consumer, unencumbered by costly middlemen and distribution channels.

■ Security is a primary concern for all companies doing business over the Internet.

■ At this point, a tremendous range of business activities are being conducted over the Internet. For example, you can purchase a car online, order books on a bookstore's Web page, or order groceries for delivery to your door.

NORTON Online

To visit the
**commercial sites
described here**, visit
this book's Web site at
www.glencoe.com/norton/online

Amazon.com is the largest
bookstore on the Internet.

HANDS On Activities

USING THE INTERNET

Chapter 8 of the Interactive Browser Edition not only explains the basic principles on which the Internet works, but describes each of the key features of the Internet, including electronic mail, the World Wide Web, and other services.

The following sections are designed to help you navigate Chapter 8. As you work through the chapter, be sure to answer the review questions on the following pages. Write your answers directly in this book.

Background and History: An Explosion of Connectivity

For many people, the existence of the Internet came as a surprise during the early 1990s. The Internet, however, had actually existed for years before the development of the World Wide Web—the event which eventually thrust the Internet into the limelight. This section of the chapter describes the origins of the Internet, and the reasons behind its creation.

From the navigation menu on the left side of your browser window, choose Background and History: An Explosion of Connectivity. As you work through this section, answer the following questions:

1. Describe the purpose of the Internet, as it was originally envisioned by the Department of Defense.

_____

_____

_____

2. The Internet was originally created under the name of _____ .

3. The central structure that connects the elements of a network is called the network's _____ .

How the Internet Works

In its most fundamental form, the Internet is simply a number of computers that are connected to one another, typically by telephone lines or dedicated data lines. In order for the computers to communicate with one another, however, a number of things must fall into place. First, they must speak the same language, in the form of a network protocol. Second, the computers must have a way of finding each other across the network, so that when data leaves one computer, it eventually ends up on the computer that was intended to receive it. Third, there must be an easy way for people to identify different computers—and other people—on the Internet.

This section explains these fundamental technologies, which enable the Internet to function.

From the navigation menu on the left side of your browser window, choose How the Internet Works. Use this menu item's options to explore this section of the chapter. As you work through this section, answer the following questions:

1. All computers use the same set of protocols in order to communicate over the Internet. In basic terms, "protocols" can be described as

_____

_____

_____

_____

2. What does the abbreviation TCP/IP stand for?

_____

3. Why is the Internet often described as a "network of networks"?

_____

_____

_____

_____

4. What are the two components of the Internet that form its core?

_____

_____

_____

5. What is the purpose of an IP address?

_____

_____

_____

6. The _____ provides a system of word-based addresses rather than numerical addresses, to make the Internet easier for people to use.

7. If you visit an Internet site with the DNS address *microsoft.products.com*, what would you expect to find, and why?

_____

_____

_____

_____

8. How would you interpret the address *bjones@ibm.com*?

_____

_____

_____

_____

9. Does your school have an Internet site? If so, what is its domain name? Do you have an e-mail account at your school? If so, what is your e-mail address? If you don't have an e-mail account at your school, what would your address be if you did? How would you interpret your e-mail address?

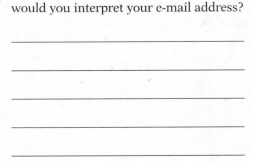

_____

_____

_____

_____

From the list of options under How the Internet Works, choose Self Check: Sending E-Mail. Complete the quiz on screen, following the instructions as you go.

Major Features of the Internet

There are many different ways to access information over the Internet. Today, most people know something about the World Wide Web, with its graphics, colors, and special navigation tools. Before the Web became so popular, however, many people found information, files, and programs on the Internet by using several other services. All those services remain active today and are still widely used. This section describes each of the information-sharing and information-retrieval features of the Internet, and explains the purpose of each.

From the navigation menu on the left side of your browser window, choose Major Features of the Internet. Use this menu item's options to explore this section of the chapter. As you work through this section, answer the following questions:

Chapter 8
Hands-On Activities

1. What is meant by the term "virtual community" on the Internet? What kind of virtual community would you be interested in joining online?

_____

_____

_____

2. The single most common use of the Internet is _____.

3. What is a news group?

_____

_____

_____

4. To participate in a news group, you must run a(n) _____.

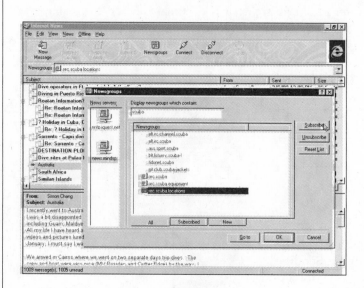

5. What is an FAQ?

_____

_____

_____

_____

_____

_____

6. _____ enables you to use one computer to control another computer over the Internet.

7. What does FTP stand for, and what does it enable you to do?

_____

_____

_____

8. _____ is a search-able index of FTP archives, which you can use to help locate a specific file's location.

9. _____ organizes directories of documents, images, programs, public Telnet hosts, and other Internet resources into logical menus.

10. Why would someone want to use the Veronica service?

_____

_____

_____

_____

_____

11. What advantages does Internet Relay Chat offer over e-mail?

_____

_____

_____

_____

_____

12. The World Wide Web is based on hypertext documents. What does hypertext enable you to do while you are using the Web?

_____

_____

_____

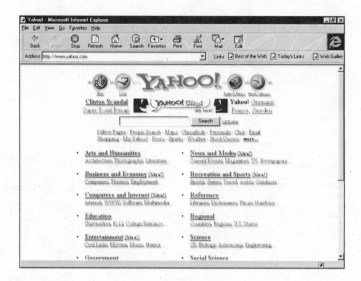

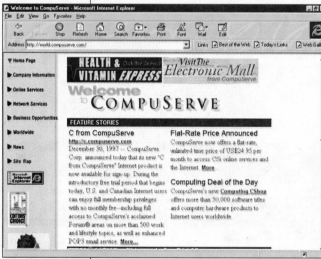

13. The address *http://www.sun.com* is an example of a(n)

_____.

14. List two kinds of services you can access by subscribing to an online service, such as America Online or Prodigy.

_____

_____

_____

_____

_____

_____

15. Online services offer

_____ , which are similar to Internet news groups, and

_____ , which are similar to Internet Relay Chat.

From the list of options under Major Features of the Internet, choose Self Check: Matching. Complete the quiz on screen, following the instructions as you go.

Productivity Tip

Now, review this chapter's Productivity Tip section, which discusses methods for conducting research on the Internet. Thinking in terms of your own school work or profession, do you think you will ever need to use the Internet to find information about a particular topic or person? What type of information would you most likely need to find?

_____

_____

_____

Accessing the Internet

Ironically, the hardest part of using the Internet is getting connected in the first place. The process is gradually becoming easier as software products are improved and more service providers emerge. But the process still requires some decisions, the acquisition of the right software, and working with an Internet Service Provider (ISP) or LAN administrator to make the connection work. This section describes the most commonly used methods for connecting a PC to the Internet, whether the PC is a stand-alone system or part of a network.

From the navigation menu on the left side of your browser window, choose Accessing the Internet. Use this menu item's options to explore this section of the chapter. As you work through this section, answer the following questions:

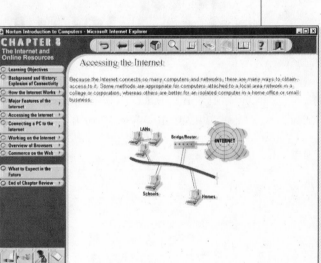

1. In a(n) _____ , Internet programs run on the local computer, which uses TCP/IP protocols to exchange data with another computer through the Internet.

2. _____ and _____ are two methods for creating a direct Internet connection over a phone line.

3. List two types of services you can purchase from an Internet Service Provider.

_____

_____

_____

_____

4. Why would an individual computer user access the Internet through an ISP rather than by connecting directly to the Internet?

_____

_____

_____

_____

5. When connecting to the Internet over a modem, what is the advantage of using a TCP/IP connection rather than a shell account?

_____

_____

_____

_____

_____

Now, review this chapter's Norton Notebook section, which discusses push technology. If you had access to a continuous Internet connection, would you want to have information "pushed" to your PC all the time? If so, what types of information would you want to receive?

_____

_____

_____

_____

_____

_____

_____

_____

_____

Connecting a PC to the Internet

After you have determined the best means of accessing the Internet, one more step usually must be taken. That is, the PC needs special software that enables it to "speak" the TCP/IP protocols required of all computers on the Internet.

From the navigation menu on the left side of your browser window, choose Connecting a PC to the Internet. Use this menu item's options to explore this section of the chapter. As you work through this section, answer the following questions:

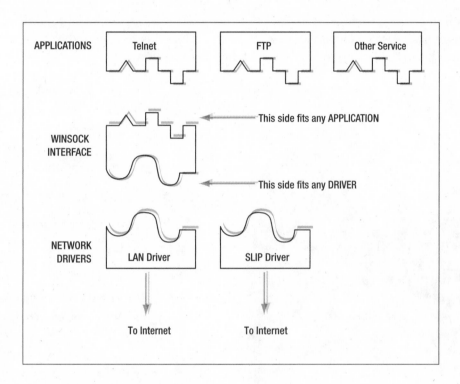

APPLICATIONS   Telnet   FTP   Other Service

◄—— This side fits any APPLICATION

WINSOCK INTERFACE

◄—— This side fits any DRIVER

NETWORK DRIVERS   LAN Driver   SLIP Driver

To Internet   To Internet

1. What does the Windows Sockets interface do?

_____

_____

_____

_____

2. If you purchase a set of Internet access tools from an Internet Service Provider, what sorts of tools can you expect the package to contain?

_____

_____

_____

_____

Chapter 8
Hands-On Activities

Working on the Internet

With Internet access being inexpensive and plentiful (you can log on virtually any time, or log on once and simply never log off), an ever-increasing number of people are using the Internet in the workplace. Whether it is for e-mail, to check stock quotes, or to do online research, more business desktops are "wired" to the Internet every day.

This growth in business use of the Internet has not been without problems. In fact, an entirely new class of business problems has arisen because of our growing reliance on the Internet. This section introduces some of these important issues.

From the navigation menu on the left side of your browser window, choose Working on the Internet. Use this menu item's options to explore this section of the chapter. As you work through this section, answer the following questions:

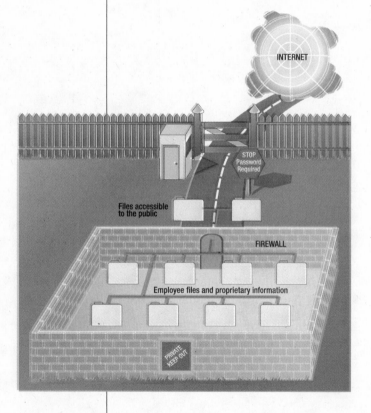

1. What does a firewall do, and why do companies use firewalls to protect their networks?

_____

_____

_____

_____

2. As more businesses begin selling products over the Internet, they must deal with two important issues. What are those issues?

_____

_____

_____

_____

_____

_____

3. For individuals who want to post materials on the Internet, three legal issues are important. What are those issues?

_____

_____

_____

_____

Techview

Now, review this chapter's Techview section, which introduces some of the many Internet-related terms and technologies that have recently emerged. Were any of these terms familiar to you before you read this section? If so, where did you hear about them? Now that you have read about them, was your previous understanding of them correct, or has it changed?

_____

_____

_____

Overview of Browsers

Shortly after the World Wide Web started becoming popular, it seemed as though everyone was developing a browser. Soon, there were more browsers on the market than word processors. Most were based on the original Mosaic technology, and therefore were very similar. In 1996, however, a few browsers began to pull away from the pack—most notably Netscape's Navigator, which eventually captured the majority of the browser market. Soon, Microsoft began to gain market share, and its Explorer product now controls an estimated 20–30 percent of the browser market.

Today, although several fine browsers are still on the market, most people use either the Netscape or Microsoft browser. This section briefly reviews both browsers and lists their capabilities.

From the navigation menu on the left side of your browser window, choose Overview of Browsers. Use this menu item's options to explore this section of the chapter. As you work through this section, answer the following questions:

1. List three components of Netscape Communicator.

_____

_____

_____

2. Name one feature that Internet Explorer 4.0 offers that is not available in Netscape Communicator 4, and then name a feature that Communicator offers that Explorer does not.

_____

_____

_____

_____

3. What is the single biggest difference between Internet Explorer and Communicator?

_____

_____

_____

_____

_____

_____

_____

Commerce on the Web

The Internet began as a largely academic community, shared to a degree by the government and military. Over time, as universities became more involved in the Internet, students and teachers found in it a place to communicate socially, and even play games with one another. The emergence of the Web, however, has brought about the full-blown commercialization of the Internet. And while most of the activity on the Internet is noncommercial, the amount of business being conducted on the Web is growing very, very rapidly.

Many observers feel that the commercialization of the Internet is inherently good, and that the Internet can sustain itself only if it begins to generate revenues for those who put the most effort and resources into it. Meanwhile, many consumers are finding that doing business on the Web (whether buying flowers, a computer, or a house) makes life a little easier.

From the navigation menu on the left side of your browser window, choose Commerce on the Web. Use this menu item's options to explore this section of the chapter. As you work through this section, answer the following questions:

1. The big hurdle to the development of online commerce is _____.

2. Why is online security such an important issue to Internet users who want to purchase products online?

_____

_____

_____

_____

_____

_____

3. What is envisioned as the greatest advantage of online commerce?

_____

_____

_____

_____

What To Expect in the Future

The Internet is growing at such an incredible rate, and in so many ways, it is difficult to predict its future. Many observers feel that, unless radical infrastructure improvements are made soon, the Internet eventually will crumble under its own weight and will no longer be able to carry traffic at the desired rate. Others feel that those issues will take care of themselves as the government, businesses, and individuals devote more attention and resources to the Internet's development.

From the main menu on the left side of your browser window, choose What to Expect in the Future. Study the discussion, and then answer the following questions:

1. In what way do you think the Internet should be used in the future? Is it currently being used in such a way? If so, how do you think this type of usage will evolve in the next few years?

_____

_____

_____

_____

_____

2. How do you feel about doing business on the Internet? Do you feel secure in giving out your e-mail address, mailing address, phone number, and credit card information over the Web, even to a "secure" Web site? Why or why not?

_____

_____

_____

_____

_____

Computers
In Your Career

Now, review this chapter's Computers in Your Career section, which discusses the ways in which the technologies discussed in this chapter could affect your career. In the space provided here, describe the area of technology that you think might most affect your career, and explain why:

_____

_____

_____

_____

_____

_____

_____

_____

_____

_____

_____

_____

_____

_____

_____

_____

_____

_____

_____

_____

_____

_____

_____

_____

_____

End of Chapter Review

The End of Chapter Review section is designed to refresh you on the major points presented in this chapter, and to test your understanding of the information.

From the navigation menu on the left side of your browser window, choose End of Chapter Review. Use the menu item's options to review the Visual Summary sections for this chapter, review the chapter's Key Terms, and take the end-of-chapter quizzes.

VISUAL SUMMARIES

Review each of this chapter's Visual Summaries in turn. Each Visual Summary provides a quick overview of the major points in each section of the chapter. If you want more information about any item in a Visual Summary, click the link button next to that item, and you will return to the full discussion of that topic. (Then choose the Go Back button to return to the Visual Summary.)

KEY TERMS

Choose the Key Terms option if you need to find the definition for any of the important terms or concepts introduced in this chapter. To get a definition for a term, simply look up the term in the list and click it. The term's definition will appear in a separate window. Use this section to prepare yourself for the Key Term Quiz.

KEY TERM QUIZ

Complete the Key Term Quiz on your screen. You complete the quiz on screen, in crossword-puzzle form. When you are done with the test, choose the Solve button at the bottom of the screen. If you want to start over, choose the Reset button to clear your responses and then start again.

REVIEW QUESTIONS

Complete the Review Questions on your screen. You complete the quiz by typing correct responses in the blanks provided, selecting responses from a list, or by selecting option buttons. When you are done with the test, choose the Done button at the bottom of the screen. If you want to start over, choose the Reset button to clear your responses and then start again.

DISCUSSION QUESTIONS

Complete the Discussion Questions on your screen. You complete the quiz by typing your answers in the text boxes provided. When you are done with the test, you can print your answers and give them to your instructor. Your instructor may choose to discuss these questions in class.

*inter*NET Workshop

Do the exercises described in the Internet Workshop section. Write your findings in the spaces provided here.

1. Did you find any other Web sites that provide information and statistics about Web usage? What did you learn from these sites? In what ways were they similar? In what ways did they differ?

   _____

   _____

   _____

   _____

2. List the names and URLs of the five new sites you found during your search.

   _____

   _____

   _____

   _____

3. List any news groups you found that were of particular interest to you. Why did you find them interesting? Do you think any of these news groups could be helpful to you in your school work or job?

   _____

   _____

   _____

4. List the names of any FTP sites you visited through your Web browser. What useful files did you find or download?

   _____

   _____

   _____

5. Were you able to set up a mail account on Hotmail or another Web-based service? How does this service compare to your normal e-mail account, through your school or ISP?

   _____

   _____

   _____

Computer Graphics and Design

Most people probably do not realize the role that computer graphics play in their everyday lives. Even if you do not work directly with a computer, you are constantly surrounded by images, designs, and products that were designed on a computer. These images and designs serve many functions, from creating an appealing impression (as a commercial or advertisement should do), to shocking or scaring the viewer (as many movies, cartoons, and television programs attempt to do), to making products perform better (as computer-designed vehicles and buildings now do).

Computer-enhanced photographs appear in many magazines each month. Most buildings are now designed on computers, as are many other products and the packages that contain them. If you have used the World Wide Web or a multimedia product (such as a CD-ROM encyclopedia or video game), you have experienced computer-generated graphics up-close.

These technological and creative advances have made computer graphics one of the fastest-growing areas of the entire computer industry, and a fascinating study of how computers can be used to enhance our education, entertainment, and quality of life.

This chapter introduces you to the world of computer graphics, from the way graphics are created in a computer, to the many applications of graphics technology. You will see how sophisticated hardware and software have changed forever the world of product design, architecture, engineering, and animation.

OBJECTIVES

When you complete this chapter, you will be able to do the following:

- List two significant uses for graphics software.
- List two significant differences between paint and draw programs.
- Name the five major categories of graphics software and list their differences.
- List five of the most common file formats for bitmap and vector graphics.
- Name three ways that computer animation is being used today.
- List and describe at least three possible applications for virtual reality technology.

KEY CONCEPTS

To have a good understanding of computer graphics, you need to learn how a computer recognizes and works with a graphic image, and you need to see the many types of software available for creating and editing graphics. The following sections break down both of these topics for you, to illustrate the many ways graphics technologies are being used.

Many traditional artists have added one or more computers to their collection of tools.

Working with Images

- Most graphics software is available for different computer platforms, including both Macs and PCs.

- Some software is available for use only on workstations. These high-performance systems are used for the most demanding graphics tasks, and are frequently used in engineering, animation, and game- and filmmaking.

- Graphics programs are designed to work with one of two types of images: bitmap images or vector images.

- Bitmaps are groups of dots—pixels—that make up an image, just like the many pixels used by your computer's monitor to display an image. Bitmaps are used by paint programs and photo-manipulation programs.

- Paint programs enable you to create individual pixels and groups of pixels. A paint program can even edit individual pixels. That is why paint programs are used for tasks such as editing photographs.

- Because they work with groups of pixels, paint programs are not well-suited to tasks such as drawing lines, circles, or text. Because the program does not recognize these objects as anything but groups of pixels, they cannot be used to edit or move the individual objects.

- A vector is a mathematical equation that describes the position of a line or other object in the program. Vectors are used by draw programs and CAD programs.

NORTON Online

For more information on **bitmaps and how they work**, visit this book's Web site at www.glencoe.com/norton/online

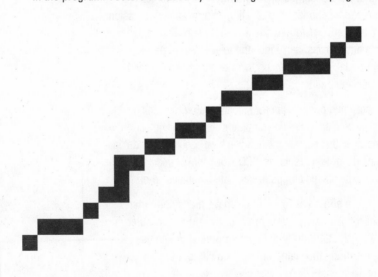

If you magnify a bitmap, you can see the individual dots that make it up.

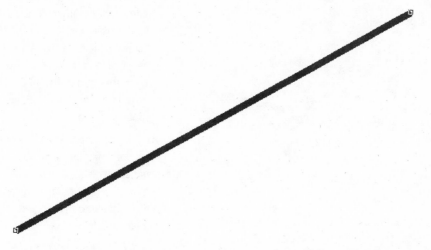

This vector is defined as a line stretching between two end-points, not as a set of dots.

- Draw programs enable you to create all kinds of geometric objects, and are ideal for creating stylized text. Because the program recognizes each object as a distinct entity, you can easily copy, move, or edit it without affecting any other object in the drawing. For this reason, draw programs are used to generate drawings of buildings, products, and other line-based or shape-based objects.

- Graphics software must store image files in a given file format. Some formats are proprietary, meaning that they work in only one or a few programs. Other formats, however, are universal and will work with many different programs.

- The most common bitmap formats are BMP, PICT, TIFF, JPEG, and GIF.

- The most widely used vector format is Encapsulated Postscript, or EPS.

- Although nearly all graphics programs enable you to create images from scratch, they are frequently used to edit an existing image, which may have been created in another program or input from a scanner, digital camera, or clip art source.

NORTON Online
For more information on graphic file formats, visit this book's Web site at www.glencoe.com/norton/online

NORTON Online
For more information on digital cameras, visit this book's Web site at www.glencoe.com/norton/online

Table 9.1	Standard Formats for Bitmap Graphics
FORMAT	**DESCRIPTION**
BMP	(BitMaP) A graphics format native to Windows and the Windows applications created by Microsoft. Widely used on PCs, less so on Macs, although the Macintosh can read BMP files with programs such as Photoshop.
PICT	(PICTure) The native format defined by Apple for the Mac. Widely used on Macs but not PCs.
TIFF	(Tagged Image File Format) Bitmap format defined in 1986 by Microsoft and Aldus. Widely used on both Macs and PCs.
JPEG	(Joint Photographic Experts Group) A bitmap format common on the World Wide Web and often used for photos that will be viewed on screen. JPEG is more than just a file format; it is a widely used standard that incorporates specific algorithms to ensure optimum image quality while keeping file size to a minimum. JPEG is often abbreviated as JPG.
GIF	(Graphic Interchange Format) A format developed by CompuServe. Like JPEG images, GIF images are often found on World Wide Web pages.
PNG	(Portable Network Graphics) A format developed as an alternative to GIF. The PNG format is still emerging, but gaining popularity on World Wide Web pages. It provides greater color quality and more color attributes than GIF or TIFF files, but smaller file sizes than JPEG.

- Scanners work in much the same
  manner as a photocopier. Instead
  of copying the image to paper, however, a scanner digitizes the image
  and stores it in a disk file, which
  can then be opened and edited in a
  graphics program.

- Digital cameras work much like
  traditional film cameras, but store
  images on disk or in a special form
  of memory rather than on film. The
  stored images can be imported into
  a computer for editing.

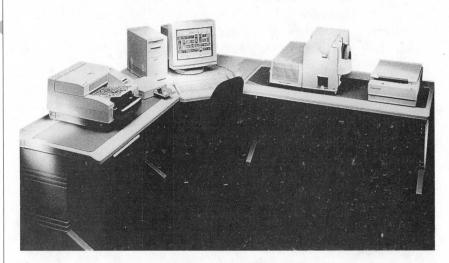

NORTON
Online

For information
on **PaintShop Pro**—a
popular paint program—
visit this book's Web site at
www.glencoe.com/norton/online

- An electronic photograph is one that was taken by a digital camera or scanned into the
  computer from hard copy.

- Clip art is existing digital artwork, such as drawings or photographs, which can be
  obtained through a variety of sources. You can load a clip art image into many types of
  programs for editing.

- Professional-quality photographs are often stored on PhotoCD.

- Copyright issues are an important concern if artwork produced by someone else is to
  be used. When using any image that was created by someone else, the user should
  always make sure that the image is not protected by copyright, which determines
  whether it can be used with or without permission from its owner.

Graphics Software

Pencil pointer

- The five main categories of graphics software are paint programs, photo-manipulation programs, draw programs, CAD software, and 3-D modeling programs.

- Paint programs include tools like paintbrushes, ink and felt pens,
  chalk, and watercolors.

- Paint programs are not well suited to applications that require a
  lot of text.

- The specialty of paint programs is to create very natural and realistic effects that mimic art produced via traditional methods.

- Photo-manipulation programs have replaced many tools a photographer uses.

- Photo-manipulation programs can exert pixel-level control over photographs and images.

- With photo-manipulation programs, photographs can be altered with no evidence of alteration.

- Draw programs are well suited to applications where flexibility is important.

- Objects created with draw programs can be altered easily.

- Draw programs work with text very well.

- Computer-Aided Design (CAD) software is used in technical fields, such as architecture and engineering, to create models of objects that are going to be built.

- CAD software allows users to design objects in three dimensions.

- Output from CAD software can appear as a wireframe model or as a rendered object, which appears solid.

- 3-D modeling programs are used to create spectacular visual effects.

- 3-D modeling programs work by creating objects via surface, solid, polygonal, or spline-based methods.

This image was created using photo-manipulation software tools that mimic the use of watercolors.

The original photograph was underexposed and appears very dark. The top part of the balloon, however, has been brightened in a photo-manipulation program.

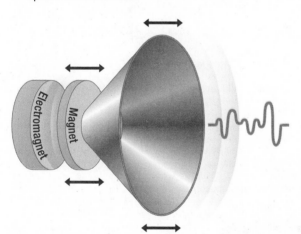

The hardware illustrations in this book were created using a draw program called Adobe Illustrator.

NORTON
Online

For more information on **Adobe Illustrator**—a popular draw program—visit this book's Web site at www.glencoe.com/norton/online

Animation

- Computers are now being used to create animations of organic and inorganic objects.

- Fly-byes and walk-throughs are basic types of computer animations.

- Character animation is the art of creating a character and making it move in a lifelike manner.

This gear is an example of a CAD model rendered with surface modeling techniques.

- Compositing tools let game- and filmmakers add characters and objects to scenes that did not originally contain them.

Virtual Reality

- Virtual reality technology is seen as the future of computer interfaces, education, and entertainment.

- Virtual reality provides an immersive multimedia experience. By combining sound, 3-D graphics, animation, and video with powerful computers, VR technology creates a virtual environment that surrounds the user.

- Wearing special goggles, gloves, and other gear, the user can move through virtual environments and interact with objects that exist only in the computer.

- Although VR is current used primarily in gaming, its potential is limitless for use in education, training, the military, and other fields.

Graphics and the World Wide Web

- Using HTML tags and simple graphics, you can easily add images to a Web page.

- On Web pages, graphics are used to illustrate content, but also are used as navigational tools and buttons.

- The JPG and GIF image formats are the most widely used formats on the World Wide Web.

- Animation can be added to a Web page by using simple animated GIF files or plug-in software, such as Shockwave.

- Emerging technologies are making it possible to add streaming video to Web pages, making them much like television.

- The VRML programming language enables designers to create immersive 3-D Web sites, filled with computer-generated landscapes, buildings, moving characters, and more.

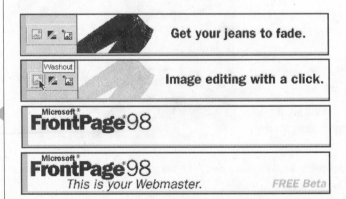

Get your jeans to fade.

Image editing with a click.

Microsoft®
FrontPage®98

Microsoft®
FrontPage®98
This is your Webmaster.   FREE Beta

HANDS On Activities

COMPUTER GRAPHICS AND DESIGN

Chapter 9 of the Interactive Browser Edition introduces you to a variety of graphics concepts and tools. As you work through Chapter 9, you will learn about the most commonly used types of graphics and file formats, devices for inputting graphical data into a computer, and many different graphics programs.

The following sections are designed to help you navigate Chapter 9. As you work through the chapter, be sure to answer the review questions on the following pages. Write your answers directly in this book.

Working with Images

Working with images is a matter of understanding your options. Which type of graphic is better suited to your needs, bitmap or vector? What format or formats can your software support? What type of graphics software do you need? This section discusses all these options and more.

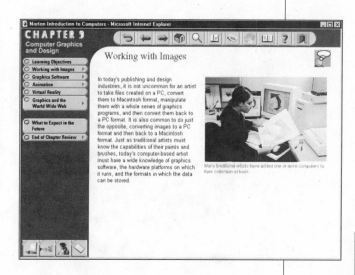

From the navigation menu on the left side of your browser window, choose Working with Images. Use this menu item's options to explore this section of the chapter. As you work through this section, answer the following questions:

1. List three reasons why the Macintosh became so popular among artists and designers in the 1980s.

_____

_____

_____

2. Workstations are typically reserved for demanding graphics applications, such as

_____ , _____ ,

_____ , and _____ .

3. Why are workstations so well suited to complex graphics and design work?

_____

_____

_____

4. Based on the reading, how would you define the term "proprietary format"?

_____

_____

_____

5. What advantage does a "nonproprietary" format provide over proprietary formats?

_____

_____

_____

Congratulations!

6. A(n) _____ image is represented as a grid of dots.

7. A(n) _____ image uses mathematical equations to describe the positions of lines.

8. A(n) _____ program works with bitmap images; a(n)

_____ program works with vector images.

9. Why is the work of bitmap-based software so complex?

_____

_____

_____

8 inches

10 inches

8 inches x 72 ppi = 576 pixels
10 inches x 72 ppi = 720 pixels

    576 pixels
x   720 pixels
414,720 pixels

ppi= pixels per inch

8 inches

10 inches

8 inches x 72 ppi = 576 pixels
10 inches x 72 ppi = 720 pixels

    576 pixels
x   720 pixels
414,729 pixels
x   8 bits per pixel
3,317,760 bits

ppi= pixels per inch

10. Three "universal" file formats used by many vector programs are

_____, _____, and

_____.

11. Three standard file formats used for bitmap graphics are

_____, _____,

and _____.

12. Using a scanner, you can _____ a printed image so that it can be imported into a computer.

13. Digital cameras work by _____

_____

_____.

14. List three advantages of storing digitized photographs on PhotoCD instead of simply scanning them and storing them on a computer's hard disk.

_____

_____

_____

15. What is clip art, and why is it important to artists and nonartists?

_____

_____

_____

16. Suppose that you have scanned a photograph from a magazine because you want to use it in a report. After scanning it, you use a graphics program to make some changes to it. Now that you have modified the image, is it yours to use freely?

_____

_____

_____

From the list of options under Working with Images, choose Self Check: Bitmap v. Vector. Complete the quiz on the screen; follow the instructions on the screen as you go.

Now, review this chapter's Norton Notebook section, which discusses digital cameras and digital photography. Do you think digital photography technology would be helpful in your career? For personal use, would you prefer a digital photography system or a traditional film camera? Do you think that digital photography technology will someday completely replace traditional photographic equipment? Explain your answers.

_____

_____

_____

_____

Graphics Software

Many types of graphics programs are available, covering a wide range of costs, features, and applications. Each category of software, however, is best suited for a particular type of graphic or design, whether you are drawing simple circles and squares, editing photographs, designing buildings, or creating animated characters.

From the navigation menu on the left side of your browser window, choose Graphics Software. Use this menu item's options to explore this section of the chapter. As you work through this section, answer the following questions:

1. The five categories of graphics software

    are: _____ ,

    _____ ,

    _____ ,

    _____ , and

    _____ .

2. Paint programs function by keeping track
    of _____ .

3. If you draw a circle in a paint program, why can't you edit or move the circle as a whole, single object on the screen?

    _____

    _____

    _____

    _____

4. List two of the special effects that can be created by using a paint program.

    _____

    _____

    _____

    _____

    _____

    _____

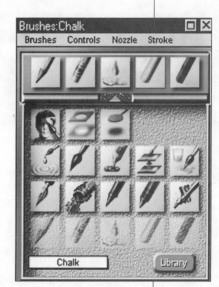

5. Is a photo-manipulation program bitmap-based or vector-based?

    _____

6. What types of tasks can you perform using photo-manipulation software?

_____

_____

_____

7. Why are draw programs sometimes referred to as "object-oriented programs"?

_____

_____

_____

_____

_____

_____

_____

8. Describe the difference between resolution-dependent and resolution-independent software.

_____

_____

_____

9. The acronym "CAD" can stand for what? _____

_____

10. Because CAD drawings are usually the basis for the actual building or manufacturing process, CAD programs must provide a high degree of

_____.

11. In CAD design, what is the purpose of layers?

_____

_____

_____

12. In a CAD drawing, 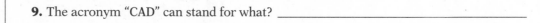 _____ are notations showing the measurements of an object.

13. What is the difference between a wireframe 3-D model and a solid 3-D model?

_____

_____

_____

_____

_____

_____

14. When a 3-D model is _____,
its solid parts are shaded, creating output that looks almost real.

15. Briefly describe how the four types of 3-D modeling software work:

■ Surface modelers _____

_____

_____

■ Solids modelers _____

_____

_____

■ Polygonal modelers _____

_____

■ Spline-based modelers _____

_____

From the list of options under Graphics Software, choose Self Check: Graphics Software Programs. Complete the quiz on the screen; follow the instructions on the screen as you go.

Animation

Animation isn't just for Saturday morning cartoons any more. Using powerful computers and software, animators are creating fully animated commercials, TV shows, and movies. A movie may be populated with nothing but animated characters, or individual characters may be blended with real actors. An animator can create a complete three-dimensional character which, like a puppet, can be bent, twisted, and moved in the same ways as its real-life counterpart. Using the computer, inanimate objects—like cars and boxes—can be made to dance like people or crawl like snakes.

From the navigation menu on the left side of your browser window, choose Animation. Use this menu item's options to explore this section of the chapter. As you work through this section, answer the following questions:

1. Both traditional and computer-generated animations are created from a series of images, called _____.

2. A(n) _____ image looks so realistic that it could be mistaken for a photograph of a real-life object.

3. What is the difference between a fly-by and a walk-through?

_____

_____

 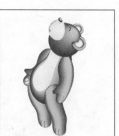   

4. _____ is the art of creating a character (such as a person, an animal, or even a nonorganic thing, such as a box or car) and making it move in a lifelike manner.

5. In what ways have computers simplified the character-animation process?

_____

_____

6. In the _____ process, computer-generated imagery is blended with filmed or videotaped images of real characters and objects.

 Techview

Now, review this chapter's Techview section, which discusses some of the advanced animation techniques that are being used in movies and television. People typically think of entertainment applications for such technology, but what other possible uses may it have? List at least one nonentertainment application for advanced animation technology, and describe how it might be used in that application.

_____

_____

Virtual Reality

Imagine taking flying lessons without leaving the ground. Or touring your new house before it has been built. These are just two of the possibilities offered by virtual reality (VR) technology. VR combines the full range of multimedia technology—video, sound, 3-D graphics, and others—and combines them with powerful computers to create fully immersive multimedia experience. This means you are actually part of the virutal environment, moving through rooms or landscapes that exist only in the computer.

From the navigation menu on the left side of your browser window, choose Virtual Reality. As you work through this section, answer the following questions:

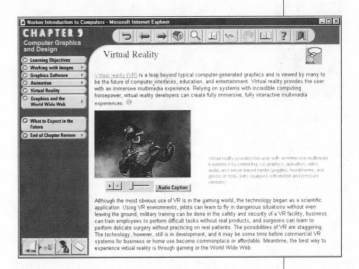

1. Using true virtual reality, you become part of a(n) _____ .

2. What is meant by "six degrees of freedom" in virtual reality?

_____

_____

_____

3. List one possible future use for virtual reality technology, aside from gaming.

_____

_____

_____

_____

Graphics and the World Wide Web

Because it is an easy task to post pages on the World Wide Web, businesses and individuals are creating thousands of new Web pages every day. And because graphics make Web pages more inviting and easier to navigate, people are delving into graphics like never before. Fortunately, the tools exist to help even novice artists create professional-looking graphics for use on the Web. This section introduces the ways in which illustrations and photographs are used on the Web.

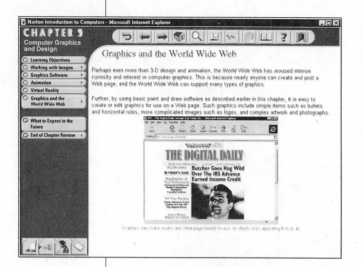

From the navigation menu on the left side of your browser window, choose Graphics and the World Wide Web. Use this menu item's options to explore this section of the chapter. As you work through this section, answer the following questions:

1. Most Web pages are actually collections of separate _____ and

_____.

2. If graphics make Web pages more appealing, why do many Web users exit from a page that includes large images?

_____

_____

_____

_____

3. Generally, Web designers try to limit their color depth to _____ bits, or _____ colors.

4. Web designers stick to the GIF and JPEG file formats when adding graphics to Web pages. What are these two file formats used for?

_____

_____

_____

5. _____ are frequently used in advertising banners and other graphic elements where the user's attention is desired.

6. What does VRML enable a Web designer to do?

_____

_____

_____

From the list of options under Graphics and the World Wide Web, choose Self Check: Graphics and the World Wide Web. Complete the quiz on the screen; follow the instructions on the screen as you go.

Productivity Tip

Now, review this chapter's Productivity Tip section, which discusses the many graphics programs available that can help even a nonartist create effective graphics. Think for a moment of your own graphics needs. In your career or schoolwork, what types of graphics programs might be most helpful to you? Do you think you might need to develop advanced graphics skills? Why or why not?

_____

_____

_____

_____

_____

_____

_____

_____

_____

What To Expect in the Future

Today's graphics technology enables designers and artists—and everyday home users—to create images and effects that simply were not possible a decade ago. If the trends continue, what graphical magic will designers be able to perform ten years from now? It can be hard to imagine what is coming next.

From the navigation menu on the left side of your browser window, choose What to Expect in the Future. Study the discussion and answer the following questions:

1. Programs like PaintShop Pro, CorelDRAW, and others have brought sophisticated graphics capabilities to home users, at affordable prices. As casual computer users begin designing their own Web pages and gain the ability to record their own compact disks, what other types of graphics capabilities might home users require? How advanced do you think casual users will eventually become in the use of graphics?

   _____

   _____

   _____

2. Computer-generated graphics have spawned a new breed of film and game entertainment. Many amusement parks now have "3-D thrill rides" based on computer-generated graphics and special effects. What will come next, in your opinion? In what field of entertainment will computer graphics emerge next, and what effect will it have on consumers?

   _____

   _____

   _____

Computers
In Your Career

Now, review this chapter's Computers in Your Career section, which discusses the ways in which the technologies covered in this chapter could affect your career. In the space provided here, describe the area of technology that you think might most affect your career, and explain why:

_____

_____

_____

_____

_____

End of Chapter Review

The End of Chapter Review section is designed to refresh you on the major points presented in this chapter, and to test your understanding of the information.

From the navigation menu on the left side of your browser window, choose End of Chapter Review. Use the menu item's options to review the Visual Summary sections for this chapter, review the chapter's Key Terms, and take the end-of-chapter quizzes.

VISUAL SUMMARIES

Review each of this chapter's Visual Summaries in turn. Each Visual Summary provides a quick overview of the major points in each section of the chapter. If you want more information about any item in a Visual Summary, click the link button next to that item, and you will return to the full discussion of that topic. (Then choose the Go Back button to return to the Visual Summary.)

KEY TERMS

Choose the Key Terms option if you need to find the definition for any of the important terms or concepts introduced in this chapter. To get a definition for a term, simply look up the term in the list and click it. The term's definition will appear in a separate window. Use this section to prepare yourself for the Key Term Quiz.

KEY TERM QUIZ

Complete the Key Term Quiz on your screen. You complete the quiz on screen, in crossword-puzzle form. When you are done with the test, choose the Solve button at the bottom of the screen. If you want to start over, choose the Reset button to clear your responses and then start again.

REVIEW QUESTIONS

Complete the Review Questions on your screen. You complete the quiz by typing correct responses in the blanks provided, selecting responses from a list, or by selecting option buttons. When you are done with the test, choose the Done button at the bottom of the screen. If you want to start over, choose the Reset button to clear your responses and then start again.

DISCUSSION QUESTIONS

Complete the Discussion Questions on your screen. You complete the quiz by typing your answers in the text boxes provided. When you are done with the test, you can print your answers and give them to your instructor. Your instructor may choose to discuss these questions in class.

*inter*NET Workshop

Do the exercises described in the Internet Workshop section. Write your findings in the spaces provided here.

1. How many Web sites did you find providing information on 3-D design, CAD, and computer animation? Did you find information about unique applications for these technologies? If so, what are they?

_____

_____

_____

_____

_____

_____

2. List the names and URLs of sites you found that take advantage of the Shockwave plug-in. What could you do at each site that was not possible at other sites?

_____

_____

_____

_____

_____

3. List the VRML sites that you found on the Web. What were they like? Did you find their content compelling? Did the VRML adaptations make the sites more interesting, exciting, or informative?

_____

_____

_____

_____

_____

The New Media

OBJECTIVES

When you complete this chapter, you will be able to do the following:

■ **Define the term "interactive media" and describe its role in new communications technologies.**

■ **List three ways consumers receive multimedia content.**

■ **Give one example of multimedia applications in each of these three areas: schools, businesses, and homes.**

■ **Define the term "hypermedia" and describe its role in multimedia presentations.**

■ **Name three ways in which you might use virtual reality.**

■ **Explain one way in which digital convergence has affected the media being produced for mass consumption.**

People have always used one medium or another (speech, text, pictures, animation, and so on) to communicate messages and convey information. As technologies enabled them to do so, people began combining different media to communicate more effectively. As technologies improved, multimedia—the use of several types of media at one time—became more common, until now it is part of everyday life.

Consider television, a communication technology that brings us sounds, still pictures, video, animations, and text. Various combinations of these media are used to create messages with different types of impact—to inform, to entertain, to persuade, and to sell.

Computers have taken multimedia to a new level, however, by empowering the audience to respond directly to the message, and even to control its direction or change its content. This message-response phenomenon is called interactivity. Multimedia programs that enable the user to interact are called interactive multimedia. This type of programming has enjoyed stunning growth in the past few years, in the form of video and online games, entertainment and educational software, and even new forms of interactive television.

When these different media types converge with various communications technologies (such as CD-ROM or the Internet), the result is called new media. This chapter explores the world of new media, describes the key technologies that make new media content and delivery possible, and discusses the impact of new media on our lives.

KEY CONCEPTS

The quest for interactivity has spawned an entirely new breed of computer and communications technology, and has changed the way consumers use and think about computers. In the past decade, interactive multimedia programs have helped us work, learn, and play in ways that had never before been dreamed of. To appreciate the power of interactivity, you need to understand its underlying concepts and technologies, as well as the processes its developers use to create these fascinating programs.

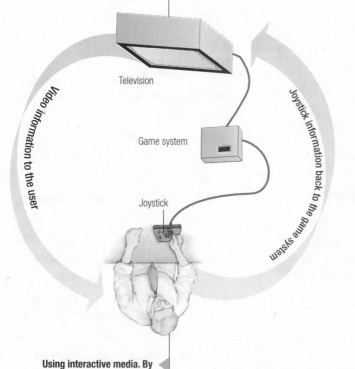

Television

Game system

Joystick

Video information to the user

Joystick information back to the game system

Using interactive media. By enabling the user to respond and control the content's direction, the program creates a feedback loop.

The Power of Interactivity

■ A medium is a unique means of conveying information. Speech is one medium, while written text is another. Others are graphics, video, animation, and audio (such as music or sound effects).

■ The term media is the plural of medium. Together, speech and text are media. When different media are used simultaneously, the result is a multimedia event.

■ If a multimedia event enables the user to respond—to change the event's direction or even its content—then the program is described as interactive multimedia. Interactivity enables the viewer to participate in the action on the screen.

■ The popularity of video games demonstrates a widespread interest among users in interacting with multimedia content. These games enable users to control the flow of content by using a pointing device, joystick, keyboard, or some other type of device.

■ Broadcast and cable TV companies are still determining how best to produce and deliver interactive material. One type of system—pay-per-view—enables the user to interact in a limited manner, by ordering a specific program for viewing. Other types, such as those used by live talk shows, enable the user to interact over a phone link or Internet connection, to provide feedback to the program.

NORTON
Online

For examples of **interactive television programs**, visit this book's Web site at www.glencoe.com/norton/online

CNN's *TalkBack Live* television show enables viewers at home to communicate with the show's guests via the Internet.

- The CD-ROM for personal computers and video games is the most popular interactive content delivery medium today. Examples include CD-ROM-based games, encyclopedias, and design programs.

- Online delivery via commercial services and the Internet is growing rapidly.

- In education, interactive multimedia can enrich the learning experience by engaging students in the content, connecting students in different locations, and simulating real-world actions and their consequences.

- Businesses use interactive multimedia for training, video conferencing, and reaching customers with catalogs and customer support.

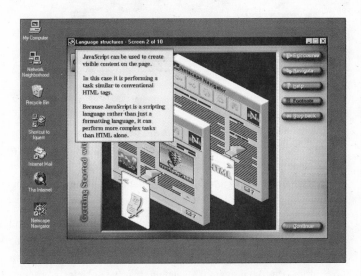

This computer-based training program is designed to teach JavaScript.

- Home reference and how-to books come alive in interactive multimedia form. These products can teach the user how to perform specific tasks (such as building a deck) or help the user with design tasks (such as landscaping), enabling the user to make selections and provide feedback.

- Entertainment is the widest application of multimedia in the home today. Someday, interactive television may allow you to order any program you want, whenever you want to see it.

The New Media

- Traditional media companies (such as the print media, music publishers, and broadcasters) are exploring new media as an opportunity to reach new markets and new audiences.

- The concept of digital convergence is at the heart of new media, and is what enables publishers and content developers of all types to deliver content in new ways. All content can now be converted into digital format, all of which can be delivered via a single delivery method, such as cable television, CD-ROM, or the Internet.

- Traditional print publishers are converting many printed products into multimedia format. Adding animation, video, and sound to what is normally print media makes it easier for many users to understand concepts.

- Publishers are quickly learning that technical wizardry is not enough to sell a multimedia program: there must be content that the audience considers valuable.

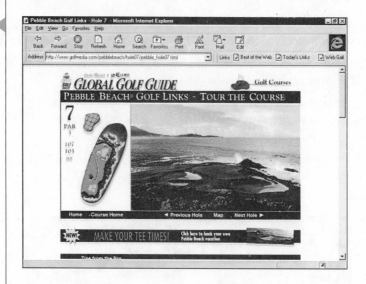

On this multimedia Web site, the Global Golf Guide offers information about golf packages, resorts, courses, and employment. The site utilizes video, audio, text, and virtual reality to guide visitors around courses.

■ To ensure that multimedia products are developed in a standard manner, and that current-model PCs can play those products, computer manufacturers and multimedia developers follow the Multimedia PC (MPC) standard. This standard, which is currently in its third revision, defines the requirements a computer must meet in order to be fully multimedia-capable.

■ High-quality content requires a great deal of storage space and bandwidth. For this reason, developers are using data compression technology to store more data or deliver it at greater speeds. Compression allows more information—higher-quality content—to reach users via existing delivery vehicles such as CD-ROM, telephone wires, and TV cable.

■ Companies that produce (or routinely use) large multimedia programs must develop or install specialized multimedia networks. Such networks are similar to normal LANs but can store and transmit much larger quantities of data without bogging down. A multimedia network can carry normal data, streaming video, and more.

■ The amount of traffic a network can handle is called its bandwidth capacity. Special software and hardware tools optimize the bandwidth capacity of multimedia networks.

■ Two widely used compression standards in multimedia are the MPEG and JPEG standards. The MPEG standard is used to compress full-motion video files, while the JPEG standard is used to compress still images.

■ Most multimedia products include a specially designed navigation system, which enables users to find their way around the content. Most navigation systems provide one or more methods for the user to control data flow or change directions within the program.

■ A hypermedia link (derived from hypertext) connects one piece of media on the screen with perhaps a different kind of media, which may even be located on another computer along the network. By choosing a hypermedia link, usually by clicking it with the mouse, the user can "jump" to a different point in the program, or to different content entirely.

■ Hypermedia links are found in many types of programs and online documents. They are commonly used in online help systems, for example, to enable the user to jump from one topic to another.

■ The highlighted links found in World Wide Web pages exemplify hypermedia.

NORTON
Online
For information on the **MPC standard**, visit this book's Web site at www.glencoe.com/norton/online

Table 10.1	Multimedia PC Level 3 Specification
CPU (Min.)	75 MHz Pentium or equivalent for hardware MPEG or 100 MHz Pentium for software MPEG or equivalent
Operating System	Windows 95
RAM (Min.)	8 MB
Floppy Drive	Yes
Hard Drive (Min.)	540 MB
Video Playback	MPEG
Two-Button Mouse	Yes
101-Key Keyboard	Yes
CD-ROM Drive	Quad speed; 600 KB per sec transfer rate; 250 ms average access time
Audio	Compact audio disk playback 16-bit digital; 44.1, 22.05, and 11.025 kHz sampling rates; microphone input; wavetable support; internal mixing of four sources
Serial Port	Yes
Parallel Port	Yes
Midi I/O Port	Yes
Joystick Port	Yes
Speakers	Two-piece stereo; 3 watts per channel

Source: Software Publishers Assn. Multimedia PC Working Group

■ Personal computers are becoming powerful enough to create and display virtual reality (VR)—an immersive form of multimedia, in which scenes and sounds are realistic enough to make you believe you are in a different place.

■ Using a programming language called Virtual Reality Modeling Language (VRML), Web designers can create 3-D web sites that offer VR-style environments for users to navigate.

▶ Common navigation methods in multimedia programs.

Creating Multimedia

- Because multimedia products are so complex, their development usually requires teams of people with different skills.

- Planning is the most time-consuming part of creating a multimedia program or presentation.

- Prior to doing any development, multimedia developers define the product's audience to understand the users' expectations and preferences.

- Before turning to the computer, multimedia designers typically sketch out an outline or storyboards of key scenes planned for the program.

- Multimedia developers can choose from a wide array of hardware and software tools, which they can use in creating any type of multimedia product. These tools are required to edit and format text, still images, video, audio, and navigation.

- After the different pieces of content have been developed, they are combined into a finished product by using multimedia authoring tools. These tools recognize the different types of media and help the developer to combine them, control the sequences in which they appear, and create an interface for the user.

- Prior to release to the public, multimedia programs are tested on a variety of hardware platforms. Developers often recruit members of the product's target audience to test the product and provide feedback about its features and performance.

The multimedia development
process involves a number of
distinct steps before achieving
a final product.

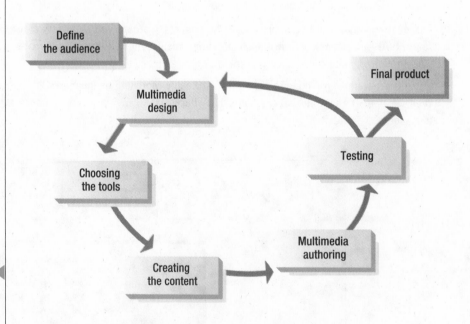

Define the audience → Multimedia design → Choosing the tools → Creating the content → Multimedia authoring → Testing → Final product

HANDS On Activities

USING AND DEVELOPING INTERACTIVE MULTIMEDIA

Chapter 10 of the Interactive Browser Edition introduces you to many types of multimedia programs, and provides demonstrations that will help you understand the concept of interactivity. You will see examples of the many ways in which multimedia content is delivered, and you will walk step by step through the process of creating a multimedia product.

The following sections are designed to help you navigate Chapter 10. As you work through the chapter, be sure to answer the review questions on the following pages. Write your answers directly in this book.

The Power of Interactivity

In the early days of window-based interfaces, interactivity was loosely defined as pointing and clicking, or simply making choices from toolbars and menus. The definition of interactivity is much broader now, reflecting the ability of users to actually direct the way a multimedia event works, change the course of action, affect the actions of characters, or revise the storyline. Until the early 1990s, any program that combined sounds and images was considered a multimedia event. Today's truly interactive multimedia products—whether they are on a CD-ROM, the Web, or some other delivery method—are free-flowing, able to change instantly to accommodate the user's needs.

Because multimedia technology has matured so much in the last few years, it is continually finding new uses in schools, homes, and business. Multimedia products are used for training, entertainment, marketing, testing, and many other applications.

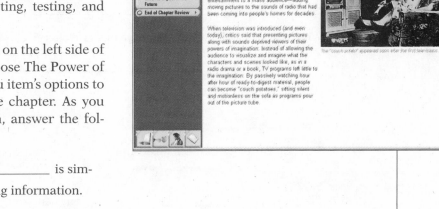

From the navigation menu on the left side of your browser window, choose The Power of Interactivity. Use this menu item's options to explore this section of the chapter. As you work through this section, answer the following questions:

1. A(n) _____ is simply a means of conveying information.

2. In its simplest form, what is a multimedia event?

_____

_____

_____

3. When one of the first electronic multimedia devices—the television—was introduced, critics complained that it would do what?

_____

_____

_____

4. Could the early criticism of television be applied to modern interactive multimedia programs? Explain your reasoning.

_____

_____

_____

5. What special capability do interactive media events give their audience?

_____

_____

_____

6. Two popular delivery mechanisms for interactive multimedia programming are

_____ and _____.

7. CD-ROM-based _____ are an example of common interactive multimedia applications used in education.

8. By using distance learning technology, Web-based _____ enable students to take classes online.

9. Companies are using CD-ROM and Web-based _____ products to educate employees about a variety of tasks and subjects.

10. A(n) _____ provides a search engine to help users find the answer to a specific question or problem.

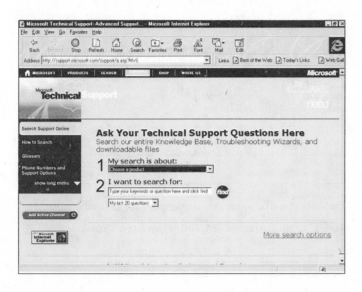

Productivity Tip

Now, review this chapter's Productivity Tip section, which discusses some of the considerations that must be made when developing multimedia content for use on the World Wide Web. If you were developing a Web page (or a site filled with them), in what unique way would you use multimedia content? How would it complement the overall purpose of your Web page?

_____

_____

_____

The New Media

With its various means of delivery, interactive multimedia is creating opportunities for many businesses, not just for well-known software makers. Multimedia is actually breathing new life into traditional publishing and media businesses, which are converting previously printed materials and old broadcast content into multimedia format.

Chapter 10
Hands-On Activities

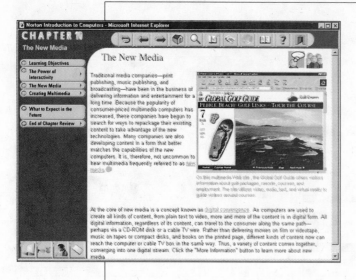

As a result, catalogs and brochures are being issued on **CD-ROM**, children's stories are being turned into games, and newspapers and radio stations are developing Internet outlets for their content.

From the navigation menu on the left side of your browser window, choose The New Media. Use this menu item's options to explore this section of the chapter. As you work through this section, answer the following questions:

1. How has the increasing popularity of multimedia products affected traditional media companies?

_____

_____

_____

2. In your own words, explain the concept of digital convergence, and describe how it can affect content providers (such as publishing companies) and consumers.

_____

_____

_____

3. The addition of _____ is one way to make plain text and pictures inviting to an audience.

4. _____ computers were the first personal computers to be equipped with the hardware required to play multimedia programs.

5. The _____ defines the minimum standards for multimedia PCs, to help multimedia developers predict how much multimedia power should be in users' computers.

6. The capacity for data transmission is known as _____ .

7. How does data compression work, and why is it helpful in multimedia applications?

_____

_____

_____

_____

8. _____ and _____ are two common multimedia data compression schemes.

9. Because interactive multimedia programs are so large, multimedia developers commonly provide a set of on-screen aids that help the user _____ the software.

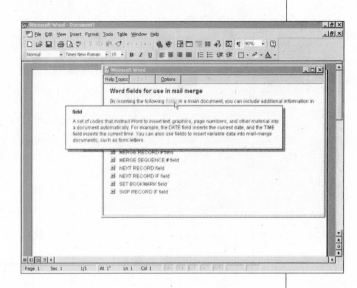

10. _____ (sometimes also called _____) allows users to click on one type of media to navigate to the same or other type of media in a multimedia environment.

11. _____ technology enables the re-creation in a computer display of what appears to be physical space.

From the list of options under The New Media, choose Self Check: User-Directed Navigation. Complete the quiz on screen, following the instructions as you go.

NORTON *Notebook*

Now, review this chapter's Norton Notebook section, which explains how new media technologies are being applied to distance learning. Would you be comfortable studying by distance learning? What if distance learning were incorporated into the classroom activities at school? Would you prefer using the technology in that manner, or would you prefer to use distance learning at home, on your PC or television? Support your answers.

_____

_____

_____

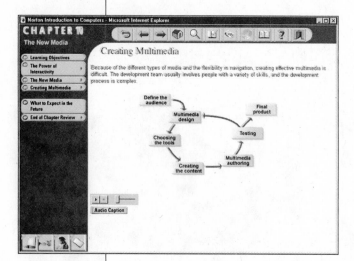

Creating Multimedia

As you might expect, the process of creating multimedia products is long and complex. Entire companies are being formed weekly to create new products, and are hiring large teams of creative and technically gifted people. From concept to finished product, a multimedia program (such as a video game, a CD-ROM encyclopedia, or the CD/book set you are now using) requires weeks of planning, design, and organization before the actual programming begins. These steps, in turn, require attention by individuals with different talents.

This section describes each of the steps involved in creating a multimedia product. Along the way, you will learn how the creative process is broken into phases, what types of tools are required, and why the developer must have a good understanding of the audience.

From the navigation menu on the left side of your browser window, choose Creating Multimedia. Use this menu item's options to explore this section of the chapter. As you work through this section, answer the following questions:

1. In order, the five major phases of multimedia development are

   _____ , _____ , _____ ,

   _____ , and _____ .

2. In your own words, describe why it is important for a multimedia developer to define the audience before actually creating a multimedia product.

   _____

   _____

   _____

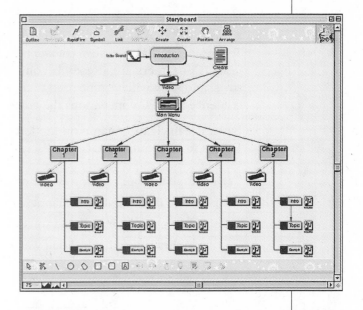

3. A(n) _____ consists of sketches of the scenes and action in a multimedia product, and is a technique used by film directors as well as multimedia developers.

4. The process of assembling different types of content into a multimedia program is called _____ .

5. During the testing phase of multimedia development, what kinds of problems must the developer look for?

_____

_____

_____

_____

_____

_____

_____

_____

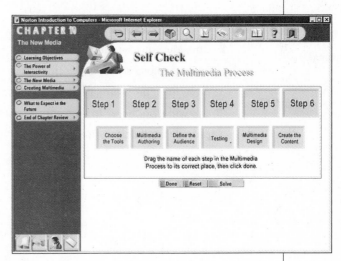

From the list of options under Creating Multimedia, choose Self-Check: The Multimedia Process. Complete the quiz on screen, following the instructions as you go.

Techview

Now, review this chapter's Techview section, which advises you on choosing the right multimedia PC. Do you currently own a PC or have regular access to one? If so, does it meet the current MPC standard? If not, what upgrades does it need? Aside from upgrades required to meet the MPC standard, are there any other upgrades you would like to make to the computer? If so, describe them.

_____

_____

_____

What to Expect in the Future

Technologies that are now considered "new media" will be commonplace in a few years. Consumers are already becoming comfortable with interactive products of all sorts, and soon will become used to finding new forms of interactivity and multimedia content in the PC applications they use every day.

From the navigation menu on the left side of your browser window, choose What to Expect in the Future. Study the discussion and answer the following questions:

1. Think about your word processor or spreadsheet package, or perhaps a presentation program. If you could add interactivity or multimedia capabilities to your favorite software package, how would you do it? How would the new features behave? How would they benefit users? What would they be used to accomplish in the program?

_____

_____

_____

2. Consider interactivity as we currently experience it. In most cases, interactivity involves making choices with a pointing device, typing commands or choices at the keyboard, or directing a program's flow with a joystick or other device. Do you think interactive control will stop there? In your mind, what is the ultimate form of interactivity? If you could provide feedback to an interactive multimedia event, how would you want to do it?

_____

_____

_____

Computers
In Your Career

Now, review this chapter's Computers in Your Career section, which discusses the ways in which the technologies covered in this chapter could affect your career. In the space provided here, describe the area of technology that you think might most affect your career, and explain why:

_____

_____

_____

_____

_____

End of Chapter Review

The End of Chapter Review section is designed to refresh you on the major points presented in this chapter, and to test your understanding of the information.

From the navigation menu on the left side of your browser window, choose End of Chapter Review. Use the menu item's options to review the Visual Summary sections for this chapter, review the chapter's Key Terms, and take the end-of-chapter quizzes.

VISUAL SUMMARIES

Review each of this chapter's Visual Summaries in turn. Each Visual Summary provides a quick overview of the major points in each section of the chapter. If you want more information about any item in a Visual Summary, click the link button next to that item, and you will return to the full discussion of that topic. (Then choose the Go Back button to return to the Visual Summary.)

KEY TERMS

Choose the Key Terms option if you need to find the definition for any of the important terms or concepts introduced in this chapter. To get a definition for a term, simply look up the term in the list and click it. The term's definition will appear in a separate window. Use this section to prepare yourself for the Key Term Quiz.

KEY TERM QUIZ

Complete the Key Term Quiz on your screen. You complete the quiz on screen, in crossword-puzzle form. When you are done with the test, choose the Solve button at the bottom of the screen. If you want to start over, choose the Reset button to clear your responses and then start again.

REVIEW QUESTIONS

Complete the Review Questions on your screen. You complete the quiz by typing correct responses in the blanks provided, selecting responses from a list, or by selecting option buttons. When you are done with the test, choose the Done button at the bottom of the screen. If you want to start over, choose the Reset button to clear your responses and then start again.

DISCUSSION QUESTIONS

Complete the Discussion Questions on your screen. You complete the quiz by typing your answers in the text boxes provided. When you are done with the test, you can print your answers and give them to your instructor. Your instructor may choose to discuss these questions in class.

*inter*NET Workshop

Do the exercises described in the Internet Workshop section. Write your findings in the spaces provided here.

1. Which Web sites did you find that provide multimedia content beyond text and graphics? List their names and URLs here, and describe the type of content they provide.

_____

_____

_____

_____

_____

_____

2. Which Web sites did you find that provide online demos or versions of interactive games or other multimedia products? Were you able to use the product online? If so, how do you think the product's online performance (speed, graphics, sound, etc.) compares to a CD-ROM version?

_____

_____

_____

_____

_____

_____

3. How many multimedia-related job opportunities did you find on the Web? List three of them here, along with the name of the company and the types of products or services it provides. Which job opportunities interest you most? Why?

_____

_____

_____

_____

_____

_____

Assignment Record

Instructor   Office Number

Office Hours

Phone   E-Mail

Midterm Date   Final Date

	ASSIGNMENT DUE	SCORE	QUIZ DATE	SCORE	TEST DATE	SCORE
CHAPTER 5						
CHAPTER 6						
CHAPTER 7						
CHAPTER 8						
CHAPTER 9						
CHAPTER 10						
PART 2 QUIZ						
PART 2 TEST						

APPENDICES

The History of Microcomputers

OVERVIEW

Computers have been around for more than 50 years, and have changed immensely in that time. The changes have been so great, in fact, that most people probably would not even recognize the earliest computers for what they were. They were giants with names like ENIAC and UNIVAC, that filled large rooms (or small buildings) but had less power than today's pocket calculators. Microprocessors were a distant dream; those old systems ran on glowing vacuum tubes like the ones that powered old radios and television sets. Many computing functions were mechanical rather than electrical, requiring punch cards and other clunky devices for input. Innovations such as video monitors and keyboards would take years to develop.

Computer scientists, however, made huge strides during the next few decades. During the 1950s and 1960s, concepts such as computer memory and long-term storage became realities, although they were very different from their current form. Operating systems were created to help control the machines, which gradually became more powerful and reliable. Programming languages were born—freeing computer users from having to enter the same instructions each time they wanted the system to perform an operation.

As computer systems improved, people began thinking of new uses for them. Government agencies began using them to track populations and collect taxes. The military wanted them to calculate missile trajectories and handle payrolls. Large corporations wanted them to maintain billing systems and customer lists.

Computers did not really enter mainstream life, however, until the 1970s, with the invention of the microprocessor. This discovery led to rapid development in many areas, making computers smaller and more affordable—yet more powerful—than ever. Computers and software could now be mass-produced, and "home computer" became a household word.

It is now estimated that more than 40 percent of all homes in the U.S. have at least one PC. The PC is ubiquitous in businesses, found in nearly every office and factory. The growth continues and technology development moves forward with breathtaking speed.

In this appendix, you will explore the last two decades in the history of the computer.

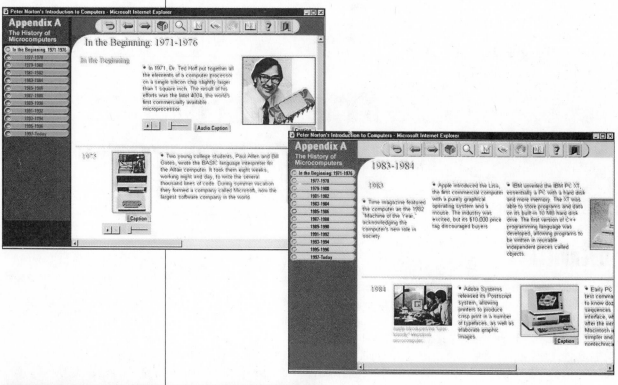

In the Beginning: 1971-1976

In the Beginning

- In 1971, Dr. Ted Hoff put together all the elements of a computer processor on a single silicon chip slightly larger than 1 square inch. The result of his efforts was the Intel 4004, the world's first commercially available microprocessor.

Audio Caption

Caption

1975

- Two young college students, Paul Allen and Bill Gates, wrote the BASIC language interpreter for the Altair computer. It took them eight weeks, working night and day, to write the several thousand lines of code. During summer vacation they formed a company called Microsoft, now the largest software company in the world.

Caption

1983-1984

1983

- Time magazine featured the computer as the 1982 "Machine of the Year," acknowledging the computer's new role in society.

- Apple introduced the Lisa, the first commercial computer with a purely graphical operating system and a mouse. The industry was excited, but its $10,000 price tag discouraged buyers.

- IBM unveiled the IBM PC XT, essentially a PC with a hard disk and more memory. The XT was able to store programs and data on its built-in 10 MB hard disk drive. The first version of C++ programming language was developed, allowing programs to be written in reusable independent pieces called objects.

1984

- Adobe Systems released its Postscript system, allowing printers to produce crisp print in a number of typefaces, as well as elaborate graphic images.

- Early PC text comma to know doz sequences interface, w after the intr Macintosh i simpler and nontechnica

Caption

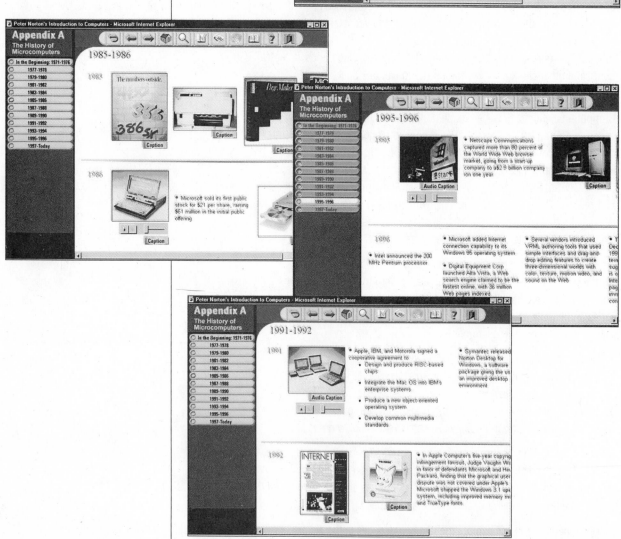

1985-1986

1985

The numbers outside.

386sx

Caption

Caption

1986

- Microsoft sold its first public stock for $21 per share, raising $61 million in the initial public offering.

Caption

1995-1996

1995

- Netscape Communications captured more than 80 percent of the World Wide Web browser market, going from a start-up company to a $2.9 billion company in one year.

Audio Caption

Caption

1996

- Intel announced the 200 MHz Pentium processor.

- Microsoft added Internet connection capability to its Windows 95 operating system.
- Digital Equipment Corp. launched Alta Vista, a Web search engine claimed to be the fastest online, with 36 million Web pages indexed.

- Several vendors introduced VRML authoring tools that used simple interfaces and drag-and-drop editing features to create three-dimensional worlds with color, texture, motion video, and sound on the Web.

1991-1992

1991

- Apple, IBM, and Motorola signed a cooperative agreement to
  - Design and produce RISC-based chips
  - Integrate the Mac OS into IBM's enterprise systems
  - Produce a new object-oriented operating system
  - Develop common multimedia standards

- Symantec released Norton Desktop for Windows, a software package giving the us an improved desktop environment

Audio Caption

1992

- In Apple Computer's five-year copying infringement lawsuit, Judge Vaughn Wa in favor of defendants Microsoft and Hev Packard, finding that the graphical user dispute was not covered under Apple's Microsoft shipped the Windows 3.1 ope system, including improved memory m and TrueType fonts.

Caption

Caption

HANDS On Activities

TWO DECADES OF MICROCOMPUTERS

The Interactive Browser Edition CD-ROM introduces you to some of the key players in the PC industry, and describes many of the most important inventions and innovations that have made the PC and microcomputer software such an essential part of our lives.

From the main menu, choose The History of Microcomputers.

The following review questions are designed to help you navigate this appendix on the CD-ROM. As you work through the appendix, be sure to answer the review questions on the following pages. Write your answers directly in this book.

The 1970s

1. The _____ was the first machine to be called a "personal computer."

2. Microsoft was formed by _____ and
_____ .

3. A computer and a company were named after a favorite snack food. What was it? _____

4. In the late 1970s, why were sales of preassembled micro-computers slow?

_____

_____

_____

_____

_____

_____

_____

5. _____ was the first commercial LAN for microcomputers, and transmitted data at a rate of

_____ .

6. In what year was Intel's 8086 microprocessor released? What did it do?

_____

_____

_____

7. The first commercial spreadsheet program for PCs was named

_____ .

8. _____ was the first commercially successful word processing program for PCs.

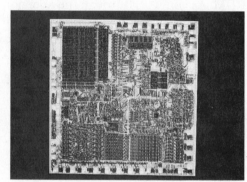

The 1980s

1. What was "Project Acorn"?

_____

_____

_____

_____

_____

_____

_____

2. Released in 1980, _____ was an integrated spreadsheet program that combined spreadsheet, graphics, and database features in one package.

3. In 1981, what could you buy for $2,495?

_____

_____

_____

4. Intel released the

_____

in 1982.

5. _____

revolutionized the architecture and

engineering industries.

6. Weighing in at 28 pounds, the

_____ was

the first "luggable" computer.

7. What was special about the
IBM PC XT?

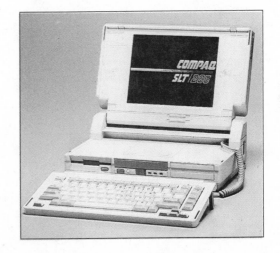

_____

_____

_____

8. What was special about the IBM PC AT?

_____

_____

_____

9. Released in 1985, the _____ was ten times faster than the 80286 microprocessor.

10. In what year did Windows debut?

_____

11. In 1987, two important new PC models were introduced. They were the _____ and the _____ .

12. _____ was the first multitasking desktop operating system.

13. What was special about the 80486 microprocessor, released in 1989?

_____

_____

_____

_____

_____

_____

_____

_____

_____

_____

_____

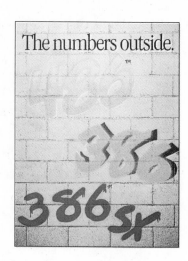

14. The creation of hypertext software led to the development of the

_____ .

The 1990s

1. What version of Windows shipped in 1990?

_____

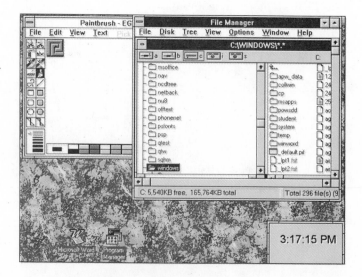

2. What was special about Motorola's 68040 microprocessor?

_____

_____

_____

3. List two of the goals of the cooperative agreement signed by Apple, IBM, and Motorola in 1991:

_____

_____

_____

4. List three important events that occurred for Microsoft in 1992.

_____

_____

_____

5. _____ , released in 1993, made the Internet accessible to those outside the scientific community.

6. What computer introduced RISC processors to the desktop market?

_____

7. What two new processors were released in 1995? _____

8. What did the introduction of VRML tools mean to Web developers?

_____

_____

_____

_____

_____

_____

_____

_____

_____

_____

_____

_____

_____

_____

_____

_____

_____

9. The number of Internet hosts had risen to an estimated _____ by 1997.

Getting Started on the World Wide Web

OBJECTIVES

When you complete this appendix, you will be able to do the following:

- **Name two means of connecting to the Internet.**
- **Name at least six important tools in a browser and describe their purpose.**
- **List four methods for navigating within a Web page or among multiple Web sites.**
- **Name one source of online assistance for using a browser or locating Web sites.**

The Internet (especially the colorful World Wide Web) is just about everywhere you look. You can find Web site addresses in advertisements for everything from movies to home appliances. People use the Internet to do serious research, to send family photos to friends, to do shopping, to play games, and to do many other tasks.

Because the Web is becoming such an essential tool, it is important that you learn to master its basic use. Believe it or not, this is a fairly simple process; once you are online, half the battle is over, and then it's a matter of learning to use a Web browser.

As you work through this book, you will find many references to sites on the World Wide Web, which provide rich sources of information and fun. That alone is reason enough to get started using the Web. This appendix will help you on your way to productive, enjoyable surfing.

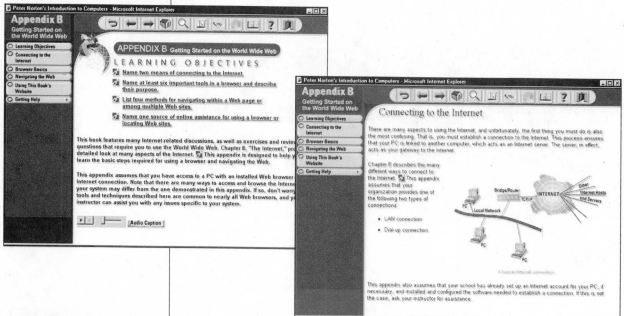

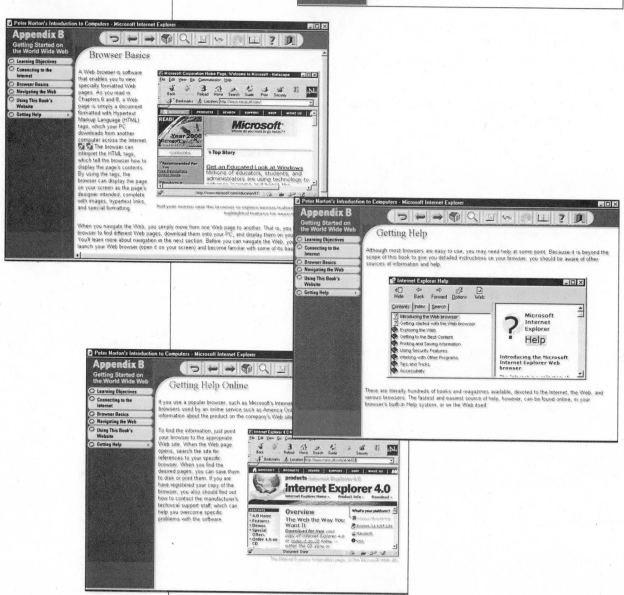

HANDS On Activities

CONNECTING AND NAVIGATING MADE EASY

The Interactive Browser Edition CD-ROM explains the basic requirements for connecting a PC to the Internet, and introduces you to several basic browser tools. Once you have established a connection and understand how to navigate the Web, you will be in for an amazing experience.

The following sections are designed to help you navigate this appendix on the CD-ROM. As you work through the appendix, be sure to answer the review questions on the following pages. Write your answers directly in this book.

Connecting to the Internet

The hardest part of using the Internet is setting up a connection—that is, unless someone else does it for you! You must start by determining what type of connection you can use.

From the navigation menu on the left side of your browser window, choose Connecting to the Internet. As you work through this section, answer the following questions:

1. Is your computer connected to the Internet? If so, by what type of connection?

_____

_____

_____

_____

2. Is a Web browser installed on your computer? If so, which browser is it, and what version?

_____

_____

_____

_____

3. Is any other type of Internet software installed on your computer (FTP software, e-mail client, and so on)? If so, list it here.

_____

_____

_____

_____

Browser Basics

As you have seen, there are many different Web browsers. Fortunately, they all work in basically the same way and provide many of the same options. In this section, you will learn about the most important browser features and what they do. Remember: even if your browser is feature-rich, you need to master only a few basic commands to successfully surf the Web.

From the navigation menu on the left side of your browser window, choose Browser Basics. As you work through this section, answer the following questions:

1. What does a Web browser do?

_____

_____

_____

_____

_____

2. What does it mean to "navigate the Web"?

_____

_____

_____

_____

_____

3. List the three basic steps required to launch a Web browser in Windows 95/98:

1. _____

2. _____

3. _____

4. To return to the previously opened Web page in your browser, you should choose the _____ button.

5. If a Web page does not load correctly in the browser, what button should you choose? _____

6. What is the purpose of a Bookmarks list?

_____

_____

_____

Navigating the Web

There are many different techniques for moving around on the World Wide Web, and any browser will support all of these techniques. This enables each user to find a favorite navigation method, making the Web a friendlier place to visit. This section introduces a few simple navigation techniques.

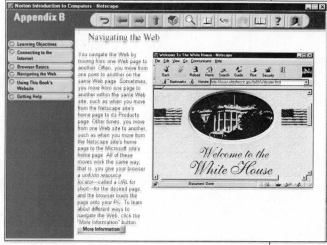

From the navigation menu on the left side of your browser window, choose Navigating the Web. As you work through this section, answer the following questions:

1. What is an URL?

_____

_____

_____

2. How can you recognize hyperlinked text, when viewing a Web page?

_____

_____

_____

_____

3. _____ and _____ are two popular graphical devices for helping users navigate the Web.

4. How does a browser's History list work?

_____

_____

_____

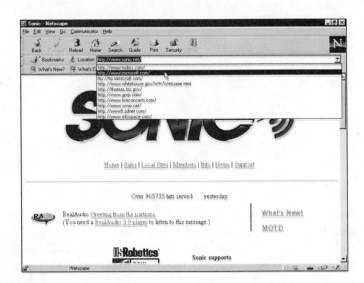

5. After practicing with your browser for a while, which navigation method do you like best? Explain the reasons for your preference.

_____

_____

_____

_____

_____

_____

Getting Help

There are many different resources that can provide help with a browser or the Web in general. It is very easy, however, to get help directly from your browser or from various Web sites. This section shows you how to find help when you need it, without looking too far.

From the navigation menu on the left side of your browser window, choose Getting Help. Use this menu item's options to explore this section of the appendix. As you work through this section, answer the following questions.

1. Does your browser feature a built-in online help system? If so, how can you access it?

_____

_____

_____

2. Using your online help system, look for information on the following topics, and describe the information you find:

■ URL _____

_____

■ Bookmark _____

_____

■ Graphics _____

_____

3. What feature of the online help system do you like best? Explain the reasons for your preference.

_____

_____

_____

4. Can you find help for your browser on the Web? Start by looking at the Web site of the company that provides your browser. (Check Microsoft's Web site, for example, for help with Internet Explorer.) What kind of information can you find there?

_____

_____

_____

_____

_____

_____

_____

_____

_____

_____

_____

5. Next, see what kind of information you can find about your browser from other sites. For example, visit a Web site such as Yahoo! or Webcrawler, and search for information about your browser. What did you find?

_____

_____

_____

_____

_____

_____

_____

_____

_____

_____

_____

_____

_____

_____

_____

_____

_____

_____

_____

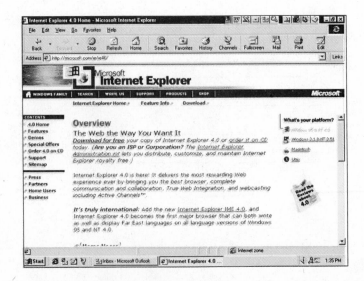

APPENDIX C

Navigating the Interactive Browser CD-ROM

GETTING STARTED

To start this program:

1_ Click the Windows Start button

2_ Go to Programs

3_ Move your mouse over the Glencoe_McGraw-Hill program group

4_ If you want to take the product tour, click the Norton Tour icon

5_ If you want to skip the tour, click the icon with the book's title. This will open the Interactive Browser Edition

When you start the program, the "loading" screen appears briefly. Then the Main Menu (or home page) opens. All the information in the program can be accessed from this menu.

NAVIGATION

When you use this product, you will always begin at the Main Menu and select a chapter. Once you are in a particular chapter, you can choose to browse through the product linearly, as you would follow a book, or you can jump from topic to topic, focusing on the subjects that interest you the most.

The Main Menu

From the Main Menu, you can go to any chapter by clicking the appropriate button. You can return to the Main Menu at any time by selecting the Home button from the toolbar. Notice that when you move your mouse over this button, the label Main Menu appears.

Learning Objectives and Links

When you select a chapter from the Main Menu, the first page that opens is the Learning Objective screen for that chapter.

Learning Objective pages include narration that introduces the concepts to be covered in the chapter. To listen to the narration, click Play on the audio playbar. If your computer does not have sound capability, you can read the audio caption by clicking the "audio caption" button.

Each learning objective contains a link to the section of the chapter that discusses that particular concept in detail. Click the highlighted text or the link icon to jump to that page. Whenever you see blue highlighted text, or the link icon, you know that clicking it will take you to a page out of linear sequence. This is one way to navigate to the important concepts in each chapter.

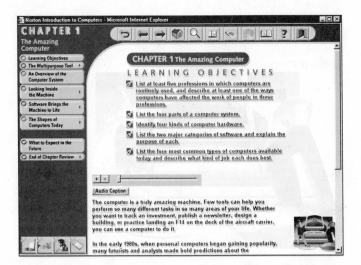

At the end of each chapter, you will find Visual Summaries that review the main concepts of the chapter. Again, each review item has a link back to the page that discusses the concept in more detail.

Web Links

You will find a special kind of link icon throughout this product. It looks like the Norton Web Site toolbar button. If you click this icon, it will take you to the Norton Web Site, for more detailed or up-to-date information about specific topics.

Note: The Norton Web links work only if you have Internet access. Also, when you click one of the Web links and jump to the Norton Web Site, you will temporarily leave the Interactive Browser Edition. Your browser will spawn a new window with the regular browser toolbars and interface. To return to this product, you must close or minimize that browser window by clicking the X on the top-right corner, and maximize the Interactive Browser Edition's window.

Chapter Navigation Menus

Another way to navigate the chapter is to use the navigation menu that appears at the left side of the screen. This menu lists all the sections of the chapter. As you move your mouse over each button on the navigation menu, notice that some sections have drop-down menus with additional subsection titles listed.

The navigation menu enables you to explore the chapter in any order you like. To jump to a main section, click the button on the navigation menu. To go to a subsection, click the title in the drop-down menu.

Notice that after you visit a page, the title in the drop-down menu changes color, so that you can identify which pages you have visited already. In the case of main sections, the indicator light on the navigation menu changes from yellow to green.

Four icons are located at the bottom of every Chapter Navigation Menu. Each icon jumps to a special topic of relevance to the chapter. As you move your mouse over each icon, the name of the section it links to appears.

Norton Notebook

TechView

Productivity Tip

Careers

Linear Navigation

Another way to navigate each chapter is to use the Next and Previous toolbar buttons to browse through each page in sequence. This method is discussed in the next section, "The Toolbar."

THE TOOLBAR

The toolbar always appears at the top of the window. Many of the functions on the toolbar are similar to those on your regular browser toolbar. As you move your mouse cursor over each toolbar button, notice that the name of the button appears.

Go Back

Previous

Next

The Go Back button takes you back to the previous screen you viewed.

The Previous button works similar to Go Back, except that the Previous button opens pages in the order preset by the chapter navigation menu.

The Next button opens the next file listed on the navigation menu.

Using the Next and Previous toolbar buttons enables you to move forward and backward through the product in a linear fashion. Rather than returning to the Navigation Menu each time you want to advance to the next page, you can simply click the Next button. To return to the previous page, click Previous. If you click a link that takes you to a page out of linear sequence, and you want to return to your former place in the product, click Go Back.

Main Menu

The Main Menu button looks like a house. Clicking this button will always return you to the Main Menu, or home page, for this product.

Search

The Search function enables you to search for all occurrences of a specific word within the product. Click the toolbar button that looks like a magnifying glass to open Search.

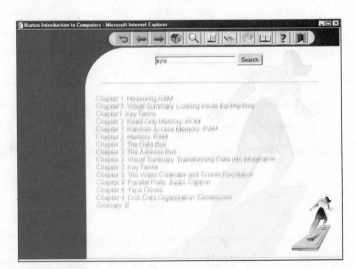

Type the word that you want to search for and then click Search. The program will return a list of all the pages that contain your search word. Click a page title to jump to that page.

Bookmarks

The Bookmark feature is similar to a browser Favorites list. To add a page to your bookmarks list, just click the Bookmarks toolbar button and then click the Add button. You can jump to any page that you previously bookmarked by selecting the page that you want from the list and then clicking the Goto button.

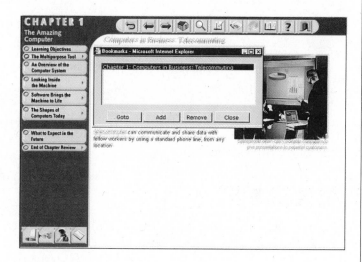

Notes

Use the Notes feature to create and save notes as you navigate through this program. Before you close the Notes window, be sure to click the Save button, or your note will be lost. You can review your notes by returning to the page where you added it and then clicking the Note toolbar button. You can either edit and save your note again or delete it by clicking the Remove button.

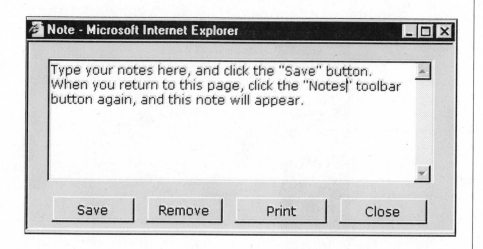

Norton Web Site

The Norton Web Site will keep you up to date on the latest information related to each chapter. If you have Internet access, you can click the Web button on the toolbar to access the Norton Web Site directly, or click the Web icon links that are found throughout the chapters.

Glossary

The glossary is organized as a dictionary of computer-related terms, with approximately 900 entries. Click the Glossary button on the toolbar to browse through all the glossary terms alphabetically. Click the link following the definition to go to the page that discusses the term in more detail.

Help

The Help section contains an interactive version of this appendix.

Exit

The final toolbar button is the Exit button. Click this button to close the Interactive Browser Edition.

INTERACTIVITIES

Throughout each chapter, you will find interactivities and "self checks." Some of the most common types of interactivities are described in this section.

Roll-Over Graphics

Many pages contain complex graphics. To get more information about specific parts of the illustration, move your mouse across the graphic. Notice that when the mouse cursor changes to a hand shape, a graphic "pops up" to provide supplementary information. When you move your mouse cursor away from the graphic, the pop-up graphic disappears.

Roll-over interactions are usually indicated by the caption "Explore this image."

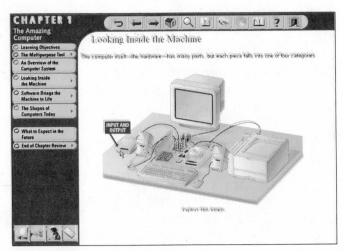

Drag-and-Drop

Other interactivities are more complex, and ask you to drag-and-drop objects on-screen. To drag an object, click the image that you want to move and hold down the mouse button while you drag the object across the screen. When you reach the area where you want to "drop" the object, release the mouse button. If you want to move the object somewhere else, just click and drag it again. When you are finished, click the Done button. To try the interaction again, click Reset. To see the correct solution, click Solve.

Crossword Puzzles

At the end of each chapter, you'll find a number of opportunities to test your knowledge. Each Key Term Quiz is organized as a crossword puzzle. To fill-in the puzzle, click the row or column that you want to solve and then type the word. Notice that as you type, the program automatically moves from block to block. As you complete the puzzle, the program skips blocks that you've already filled in. If you need help working the crossword puzzle, click the Instructions button.

OTHER TYPES OF INTERACTIVITIES

Glossary Terms

Glossary terms are indicated by green text. When you click a glossary term, a pop-up window appears with the term's definition. Notice that the glossary term's definition window disappears when you select another glossary term or click anywhere outside of the pop-up window. You can browse through the entire glossary by clicking the Glossary toolbar button.

The More Information Buttons

Some pages include a "more information" button. If you click this button, a pop-up window opens with additional text, graphics, or animations. To close this window, click the X in the top-right corner of the window.

Review and Discussion Questions

Each chapter includes multiple-choice Review Questions. Answer all the questions and then click Done to receive your score. If you want to try the quiz again, click Reset.

Discussion questions have an area in which you can type short answers. Click Reset to clear the answer boxes. You can print these questions and answers by clicking the Print button.

Printing

Some pages contain a specific Print button, but you can print any page by using your right-mouse button. Right-click on the page and select Print from the menu that appears. Be sure to right-click the text part of the page and not a graphic.

TIPS AND TROUBLESHOOTING

Installation

Problem: The Interactive Browser Edition does not recognize that you already have Internet Explorer 4.0 or Netscape Navigator 4.0 or higher installed.

With rapidly evolving Internet technologies, we could not anticipate how this product would recognize later versions of the browsers. If you know that you have the most recent version of Netscape or Internet Explorer installed, you can ignore the warning message during the installation procedure by clicking SKIP. DO NOT allow the program to install Internet Explorer 4.0 if you already have a more recent browser loaded on your computer.

If you are not sure of your browser's version number, first, open the browser. Then, click Help from the menu bar. At the bottom of the Help menu should be an entry similar to "About Internet Explorer" or "About Netscape Navigator." Select this entry. The information that appears should contain the complete version number for your browser.